PENNSYLVANIA
DISASTERS

DISASTERS SERIES

PENNSYLVANIA
DISASTERS

TRUE STORIES OF
TRAGEDY AND SURVIVAL

Karen Ivory

INSIDERS' GUIDE®

GUILFORD, CONNECTICUT
AN IMPRINT OF THE GLOBE PEQUOT PRESS

INSIDERS' GUIDE®

Copyright © 2007 Morris Book Publishing, LLC

Text design by Pettistudio LLC, www.pettistudio.com
Map by M. A. Dubé © Morris Book Publishing, LLC

Library of Congress Cataloging-in-Publication Data
   Pennsylvania disasters : true stories of tragedy and survival / Karen Ivory.
      — 1st ed. p. cm. — (Disasters series)
   Includes bibliographical references
ISBN-13: 978-0-7627-4286-8
   ISBN-10: 0-7627-4286-0
   1. Disasters—Pennsylvania. 2. Natural disasters—Pennsylvania. 3. Acci-
dents—Pennsylvania—History. 4. Pennsylvania—History, Local. I. Title.
   GB5010.I95 2007
   974.8—dc22   2006100893

Manufactured in the United States of America
First Edition/First Printing

Contents

Introduction

When offered the opportunity to write this book, I first imagined hours and hours scouring dusty books in the stacks of remote libraries. To be sure, there was some of that. But far more useful and compelling were the hours I spent turning the knobs of microfilm machines, poring over newspaper archives.

The stories behind the disasters described in these pages are largely relayed by the newspaper reporters who covered them at the time. The firsthand accounts of these tragic events were told to journalists who slogged through the floods and fire to the places where these dramas unfolded.

During the months that I was researching and writing, I was also bearing witness to the demise of daily journalism as we have known it throughout much of the past two centuries. News budget cuts. Staff layoffs. Reductions through attrition. These buzzwords mean one thing—fewer journalists on the streets, gathering the news that is the stuff of our daily lives.

The basics of a news event cannot be told by a blogger in a bathrobe. We need to know *what* happened before we can post our opinions and analysis about it. The words of eyewitnesses to history exist today only because they were told to reporters who were there at the scene—who showed up to ask, "What did you see?" "Can you tell me what happened?"

Journalism is not a cost-effective business. It costs money to send reporters out to cover a story, even more to dispatch teams of reporters to the scene of a disaster. But doing so is the only way to get the answers to the questions presented on the first day of Journalism 101: Who? What? Where? When? How?

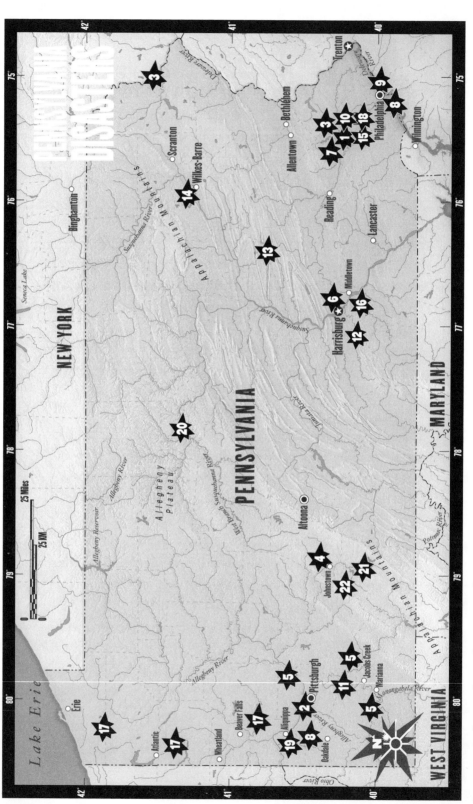

Locator numbers refer to chapter numbers.

And in pursuing these questions, journalists create what has been called the "first draft of history."

What journalists seldom find at the scene of a tragic story, however, is the answer to the question "Why?" Figuring that out often takes more time than their daily deadlines allow. For me, one remarkable aspect of researching the historic tragedies recounted in these pages was realizing that time does answer the question "why." We know now why those trains crashed, why that fire broke out, what went wrong on that plane. It's only with the luxury of hindsight that we can know "why," and take precautions to make our futures safer.

One note: Throughout this book, I have used the spelling for the city of Pittsburgh as it appears on the maps today. Though the town was founded as *Pittsburgh* in 1758, an 1816 printing run of the act that incorporated the city mistakenly omitted the *h*. For years, it was *Pittsburg*, even in the hallowed halls of the United States Post Office. The United States Board on Geographic Names even intervened in 1890, deciding that all cities and towns ending in -*burgh* should drop the *h*. In 1911 protests by Pennsylvania's historical purists succeeded in having the *h* officially restored.

"THE HORRORS WERE HEART RENDING"

The Yellow Fever Epidemic

1793

Philadelphia was a bustling young city in the summer of 1793. With a population of 55,000, it was not only the new nation's capital but its largest city, eclipsing Boston and New York in political importance. Sometimes referred to as "the Athens of America," Philadelphia was also the country's busiest port. Into this port came ships carrying cargo from around the world, as well as immigrants looking to start new lives. August 1793 in particular saw an influx of more than 2,000 refugees escaping political turmoil in the Caribbean Islands. Unfortunately, when these refugees set sail for America, they brought along an unwanted, lethal cargo: mosquitoes infected with the yellow fever virus.

Philadelphia was the perfect breeding ground for a deadly epidemic. It had been a hot summer and many commented on how bad the mosquitoes had been that year. On August 29, a letter signed with the initials A. B. appeared in the *American Daily Advertiser* in Philadelphia warning that recent rains would "produce a great increase of mosquitos in the city, distressing to the sick and troublesome to those who are well." A. B. proposed a simple method to get rid of mosquitoes: pour oil into the city's rain barrels and cisterns. But by then it was already too late. Before the first freezes of fall, an estimated 5,000 people—10 percent of the city's population—would be dead.

Dr. Benjamin Rush was an esteemed citizen of young Philadelphia. A signer of the Declaration of Independence, he was the city's leading physician, and by mid-August, he was conferring with other local doctors about an increase in

Following the mysterious epidemic we now know as yellow fever, Dr. Benjamin Rush, of Philadelphia, believed that bloodletting was an effective treatment technique. COURTESY NATIONAL LIBRARY OF MEDICINE

patients with troubling symptoms, several of whom had died. This mysterious illness started with a fever, head and body pain, and nausea. The symptoms would then frequently, cruelly disappear for several days, only to return in the form of an even worse fever and jaundiced, yellow skin and eyes. Those with the worst cases would experience skin eruptions and bleeding, followed closely by incontinence, black vomit, and frequently death.

There was great disagreement among the city's doctors over what was causing this disease and how it should be treated. Dr. Rush would conclude that the cause was a foul odor in the air, the result of a shipment of coffee from the West Indies that had been left to rot on the docks. Dr. Rush wrote to his wife almost daily during the crisis, explaining to her the difficulties in treating yellow fever:

> The symptoms are very different in different people. . . . Sometimes it comes on with a chilly fit and a high fever, but more frequently it steals on with headache, langour, and sick stomach. These symptoms are followed by stupor, delirium, vomiting, a dry skin, cool or cold hands and feet, a feeble slow pulse . . . The eyes are at first suffused with blood, they afterwards become yellow, and in most cases a yellowness covers the whole skin on the 3rd or 4th days. Few survive the 5th day. . . . Livid spots on the body, a bleeding at the nose, from the gums, and from the bowels, and a vomiting of black matter in some instances close the scenes of life.

While there was, of course, no truth to Rush's theory of the rotting coffee, word spread rapidly, and before long, the city was in a panic. Because the sickness was spreading so quickly, many assumed it was contagious and fled the city. The government shut down and members of Congress, the cabinet, and President George Washington left town. President Washington retreated to Mount Vernon, saying that he did not want to put his wife and children in danger; his departure only increased the worry of those who stayed behind. Business screeched to a halt, and most newspapers stopped publishing. Many farmers refused to bring their food into the city for fear of contracting the disease. Those with no place to go or no money to leave town stayed close to home, becoming virtual prisoners in their houses. Philadelphian Mathew Cary later wrote, "Acquaintances and friends avoided each other on the streets, and only signified their regard by a cold nod. The old custom of shaking hands fell into such general disuse that many were affronted at even the offer of a hand."

One who stayed and tried to control the growing chaos was Philadelphia mayor Matthew Clarkson. He set up a council of doctors and advisors and ordered the streets cleaned, hoping to reduce the panic. But by the middle of that September, half of the city's population had fled, and those left behind were terrified. Some stocked up on gunpowder, vinegar, and other simple disinfectants, hoping for protection; others tried hanging tarred ropes throughout their houses or wearing camphor bags around their necks. Many people tried lighting fires in front of their homes, hoping to purify the air. But there was little to calm the public. People walked in the middle of the street to avoid infected homes. There were even stories of husbands abandoning their wives, and parents leaving sick children behind.

At the end of August, Mayor Clarkson designated that Bush Hill, Andrew Hamilton's former estate on the city's

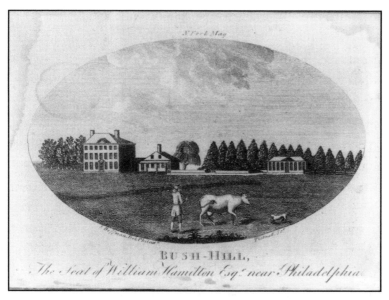

Bush Hill, the former estate of Andrew Hamilton, was converted into a
"fever hospital" where the diseased could be isolated. This illustration appeared
in New York Magazine in February 1793. LIBRARY OF CONGRESS, LC-USZ62-31792

northern limits, be turned into a so-called "fever hospital,"
hoping that isolating the sick would slow the spread of the disease. One of the Philadelphians who offered to stay in town to
help run this hospital was a French merchant named Stephen
Girard, who would later become one of the richest men in
America. He was assisted by a French doctor, Jean Devéze, a
recent refugee from the black revolt in Santo Domingo, who
had experience treating yellow fever in the Caribbean. Clarkson saw to it that several nearby bakers received enough flour
to bake bread for the patients at Bush Hill.

Many of the workers in the hospital came from the city's
black communities. It was widely—and falsely—believed that
blacks were immune to the fever. Dr. Rush and the medical

community were largely responsible for this belief, which had some legitimacy in the medical community at the time. Rush persuaded prominent black clergymen Absolom Jones and Richard Allen that blacks could assist victims without fear of contracting the disease, writing to them questioning whether the "exception . . . which God has granted you does not lay you under an obligation to offer your services to attend the sick." Encouraged by their religious leaders, many African Americans served as nurses, both at Bush Hill and in private homes, and many others were charged with caring for the dead bodies. Despite Rush's belief that blacks could not contract the disease, an estimated 240 would die during the course of the epidemic.

There was strong disagreement among the doctors caring for the ill about the best way to treat victims. Conventional medical practice at the time called for treating illnesses like yellow fever with stimulants, including wine, cold baths, and "bark," a liquid made from the bark of a Peruvian tree. Dr. Devéze at Bush Hill thought the best way to treat the sickness was to prescribe limited doses of quinine and stimulants. Dr. Rush called for a far more aggressive approach. As he said in a letter to his wife, "The common remedies for malignant fevers have all failed. Bark, wine, and blisters make no impression upon it. Baths of hot vinegar applied by means of blankets, and the cold bath have relieved and saved some. This day I have given mercury, and I think with some advantage." Rush's preferred method of treatment was purging with "heroic depleting remedies" consisting of calomel (cercurious chloride) and jalap (ground tuber from the plant).

Rush also advocated bloodletting. Via lancing, he regularly "bled" his patients of one-quarter of their blood, even four-fifths in an emergency. In his writings, Rush reported, "The

effect of bloodletting is as immediate and natural in removing
fever, as the abstraction of a particle of sand is to cure inflam-
mation of the eye . . . " Although some questioned the use of
bleeding at the time, Rush remained a staunch defender of this
practice, and it was a common treatment for many illnesses
during the time. (In fact, Dr. Rush treated George Washington's final illness in 1799 by using heavy bleeding; Washington
was dead within twenty-four hours of the procedure.) Even
more conservative doctors resorted to bleeding their patients,
and some also administered "blisters" on patients' necks and
heads and placed hot bricks on the extremities in an effort to
revive the dying.

Samuel Breck, a merchant in the city, recalled things this
way:

> The horrors of this memorable affliction were extensive and
> heart rending. Nor were they softened by professional skill.
> . . . The disorder . . . was awkwardly treated. Its rapid march,
> being from ten victims a day in August to one hundred a day
> in October, terrified the physicians, and led them into con-
> tradictory modes of treatment. . . . For a long time nothing
> could be done other than to furnish coffins for the dead.

Those left to care for their ill loved ones at home faced an
incomprehensible burden. Philadelphian Margaret Morris
wrote in a letter to her sister:

> My maid S was taken sick. We did not think her bad, as she
> had a fever only one night . . . and all went on well till the
> next day, when she began to vomit blackish stuff and the dis-
> charge downward was the same and about noon that day, a

vomiting of blood succeeded . . . I began to make experiments. I made her lick fine salt and a little alum. This made her thirsty and I gave her Elixir Vitriol, Vinegar and Water, and it stopt for 24 hours and then the bleeding returned. It came out like a tea pot and we had two large tubs full of sheets that were quite stiff.

The letter recounts Morris caring for numerous family members and friends over the course of a week, including a son.

When I returned that eve from my Debby, who was not well enough to be about the house, was told my Dear JM was ill & wishd to see me. I went there immediately & found him very ill with a raging fever. Alas—in the morning his skin was yellow as gold—a convulsion fitt & delirium deprived me of hope—yet the repetition of the powders . . . revived me again, & I was willing to flatter myself—he might recover. I watched by him till about one oclock & having been up the 2 preceding night was quite spent & as he slept quite easy, I lay down by him. . . . About 5 I awoke—& feeling his pulse, thought the fever was near gone off, & went to give the medicine but he could not take it—he spoke to me in a manner that poured balm into my wounded heart, lament the errors of his past life & had hopes of mercy—this was all I had presumed to ask for & my chastend spirit said thy will be done—a convulsion fitt followed & after that a sweet composure took possession of his features & he departed without sigh, groan or struggle—All this time I was alone.

By the beginning of October, conditions in Philadelphia had gone from bad to worse. The city was virtually shut down, with families isolated inside their homes. The mail was no longer being delivered; markets and banking houses closed. Philadelphia was isolated from the rest of the country, with the militia guarding the roads. James Graham, a Philadelphia doctor then in New York, complained in a letter that it felt like New Yorkers wanted to place guards "round Philadelphia armed with rifle guns and shooting down like black birds every affrighted citizen who would attempt to leave it." (Although Graham did get back to Philadelphia, he came down with the fever and died in October.) Even as Dr. Rush maintained an air of calm around his patients, he wrote to his wife that she should "converse with nobody now who comes from Philadelphia. Everything is infected in our city."

The only thriving commerce left was the business of death, with gravediggers in Potter's Field working around the clock. Funerals took place day and night, though often there was no one to bear witness; even family members stayed away out of fear of contagion. Other entire families had been wiped out. In one case, over the course of the epidemic, a man listed only as Collins in the records buried his wife, two daughters, a son, and the son's wife and child; after remarrying, his new wife died, as he did himself soon after.

As Dr. Rush stated in his writings about the epidemic, "On the fifteenth of October it pleased God to alter the state of the air." Successive frosts saw a decrease in the number of cases, and by early November, the epidemic was over. A white flag flew over Bush Hill, with bold letters proclaiming, "No More Sick Persons Here." People slowly trickled back into the city, with President Washington returning on the tenth of November. Businesses reopened, and ships once again docked at the ports. Congress resumed its session in December.

Though many would question Dr. Rush's methods of treatment during the epidemic, many others credited him with helping hold the city together during the crisis. None questioned his devotion to his patients. He frequently worked around the clock with little rest, as is clear in one of Margaret Morris's letters, when she writes, "I sent for good Dr. Rush & tho he was hardly able to walk he cam . . ." By some counts, there were 6,000 people sick with yellow fever at the height of the epidemic, with only three doctors well enough to care for them. Rush himself contracted the disease, though apparently a mild case, as he reported taking only two of his purgative powders and removing only twenty ounces of his blood.

His medical practice continued to thrive after the epidemic, and today Rush is known as the "father of American psychiatry." He was the first to argue that mental illness is a disease, contradicting the common belief that it was the "possession of demons." When it was published in 1812, Rush's *Observations and Inquires upon the Diseases of the Mind* was the first psychiatric textbook printed in the United States, and his likeness is still used in the logo for the American Psychiatric Association. He continued to serve on the medical staff of Pennsylvania Hospital until his death in 1813.

In the weeks following the epidemic, many sang the praises of those doctors, preachers, and volunteers who helped care for the ill during the crisis. But there was a backlash against members of the black community, some of whom were accused of stealing from those in their care or charging exorbitant amounts for their nursing services. The charges of profiteering were spelled out in a pamphlet published in mid-November, which prompted a harsh response from Absolom Jones and Richard Allen. In *A Narrative of the Proceed-*

ings of the Black People, During the Late Awful Calamity in Philadelphia in the Year 1793 and a Refutation of Some Censures, Thrown upon Them in Some Late Publications, Jones and Allen produced a meticulous accounting of payments and expenses and said:

> We feel a great satisfaction in believing that we have been useful to the sick, and thus publicly thank Doctor Rush for enabling us to be so. We have bled upwards of eight hundred people, and do declare we have not received to the value of a dollar and a half therefor. We were willing to imitate the doctor's benevolence, who, sick or well, kept his house open day and night, to give what assistance he could in this time of trouble.

Several days after Jones and Allen published their response, Mayor Clarkson issued the following proclamation:

> Having, during the prevalence of the late malignant disorder, had almost daily opportunities of seeing the conduct of Absolom Jones and Richard Allen, and the people employed by them to bury the dead—I with cheerfulness give this testimony of my approbation of their proceedings, so far as the same came under my notice. Their diligence, attention, and decency of deportment, afforded me, at the time, much satisfaction.

Subsequent summers saw the return of yellow fever in Philadelphia and several other large cities on the East Coast, though its effects were never as severe. More was known by then about how the disease spread, and many people retreated from the city at the first sign of the fever's return. An epidemic in 1798 would kill more than 1,000 Philadelphians, but that year, all but 7,000 residents fled the city. Large fields near the Schuylkill River and in Northern Liberties were given over to tent encampments for those with no place else to escape. Philadelphia made steps to improve its water system and banned trade with the West Indies during the summer months. But the damage to the city's reputation had been done. Though Philadelphia campaigned to remain the nation's capital, the federal government soon made plans to move to the new city of Washington.

It would be more than a century before Dr. Walter Reed conducted experiments proving his hunch that yellow fever was a virus spread by the *aedes aegypti* mosquito. This particular mosquito has several distinct characteristics that help explain the epidemic's fast spread that summer in Philadelphia. The *aedes aegypti* is different from other mosquitoes in that it prefers urban habitats, feeds during the day, and breeds best in relatively clean standing water. Unfortunately, Philadelphia, a hot, bustling city with many water cisterns, made for a perfect breeding ground.

A QUARTER OF THE CITY GONE

The Great Pittsburgh Fire
1845

It started simply enough, with a woman lighting a kettle flame to do a load of wash. It was a warm day and breezy—perfect for hanging laundry to dry. But something went horribly wrong on April 10, 1845. For whatever reason, the woman wandered away from her small fire, and the wind picked up the embers. The surrounding area of downtown Pittsburgh was bone dry after several weeks without rain, and the flames spread quickly.

William Johnston, who was sixteen at the time, recalled running toward calls of "Fire!" "The fire was but a short way off, in a little hut occupied by an Irish washerwoman, who in building a fire to aid her in her day's work made more of a blaze than was intended," Johnston wrote in a memoir. "I found the roof burning, and can bear witness that a few buckets of water would easily have extinguished the flames." But rather than try to douse the flames, Johnston and the gathering crowd decided to run for "an apparatus so superior" at the nearby Eagle engine house. The fire crew had already been alerted by the ringing of the church bell at the Third Presbyterian Church and was on its way, pulling the heavy ropes of a hand-pumped engine. Once connected to a fire plug, however, all that came out of the nozzle was a "weak, sickly stream of muddy water." The city's reservoir at Grant's Hill was feeling the effects of the weeks-long drought. There was little that could be done to stop the flames from spreading.

The city of Pittsburgh had grown in a haphazard way on the triangle of land at the convergence of the Allegheny, Monongahela, and Ohio Rivers. Though its rivers made it a growing industrial center and a vital link in the westward migration, the downtown area was a dense maze of houses, churches, hotels, factories, and warehouses. By the time the fire crew arrived at the corner of Second and Ferry, the flames had spread next door to the two-story wood-frame home of Colonel William Diehl and his adjacent commercial icehouse. The wind carried embers across Second Street to the Globe Cotton Factory. In the meantime, the volunteer firemen had climbed onto the roof of the Third Presbyterian Church and were doing their best to save the city landmark. Once the cornice caught fire, they made the decision to chop off the 163-foot steeple, and the church was saved.

But elsewhere, the flames were spreading fast, jumping from house to house and traveling quickly on the dry wooden roofs. William Johnston ran to his family's bookstore, where employees were spreading carpets on the roof and, as he recollected, "using salt freely, but it was soon apparent that all the salt of Sodom would not save it." The flames continued to travel eastward and within hours would engulf the city's entire commercial district.

In a dramatic account in the April 16, 1845, edition of *The Mystery* (a short-lived Pittsburgh paper that, at the time, was the country's only newspaper published by African Americans), the writers clearly reflect the sense of disaster that descended on Pittsburgh that day:

> We are called upon as one of the recorders of events to present to our readers abroad the lamentable and distressing account of the destruction of one-third or at least a fourth of the enterprising and populous city of Pittsburgh by fire! Yes, one fourth of the city of Pittsburgh, now lay in a distructive [sic] mass of ruins . . . we venture to say that in the history of fires, there never was the same extent of space of buildings burnt in the same length of time. The great New York fire of '35 was four days burning a space of *fifty acres,* and six hundred and eighty houses, and although the buildings destroyed in that memorable event, were generally larger than these of ours, yet, it was but the short space of *five hours,* until FIFTY-SIX OR SIXTY ACRES of the city were vacated, and we may venture to say *fifteen hundred* houses tumbled to the ground! The fire, as though impelled by the hand of the Destroying Angel rolled on from building to building, with the flight of a fiery flying serpent, consuming every house with the angry fury of a Vulcan, speeding its way with awful and terific [sic] progress, threatening the whole city, inhabitants and all, and only ceased its mad career in the line of the river, because there was nothing more for it to destroy, having swept every thing in its way for *one mile and a quarter!*

As the flames spread, residents tried frantically to save what belongings they could. Robert McKnight, an attorney, wrote in his diary that "drays, carts, furniture, horses, and men

This painting by William Coventry Wall depicts the total destruction of the Pittsburgh fire of 1845. The fire had devastated a twenty-four-block area, estimated at that time to represent two-thirds of the city's wealth.

. . . were running in all directions." The account in *The Mystery* reported: "Never did any event appear more like Judgment Day. People running, some screaming, others hallowing, warning the people to fly for their lives, carts, drays, furniture wagons, omnibuses, horses, and all and every kind of vehicle, crowded the streets to an excess which made it difficult for each to escape, and threatened destruction to all!" Many ran to the businesses along the river to save what they could, emptying the warehouses of coffee, sugar, cotton, paper, and more in piles on the Monongahela Wharf.

But the fire burned clear through to the river, where it consumed the covered Monongahela Bridge. In an 1885 memoir, Judge Thomas Mellon would recall that the bridge burned "like

FROM THE COLLECTIONS OF THE PENNSYLVANIA DEPARTMENT, THE CARNEGIE LIBRARY OF PITTSBURGH:
ROSS ALTWATER COLLECTION

a straw rope on fire." In the other direction, the fire spread as far as what is now known in Pittsburgh as the Bluff, where it ran out of fuel and burned itself out.

Despite the enormous destruction of the flames, in the end the fire claimed only two lives, and these were not discovered until days later. On April 22, human bones were discovered in a store on Second Street and were assumed to be the remains of a missing Mrs. Maglone, who was last seen nearby. In early May, the body of Samuel Kingston was found in the basement of a home two doors down from his. On the day of the fire, someone had seen him going toward his house, saying he was going to try to save his piano, and they suspected he became confused in the smoke and entered the wrong home.

In the immediate aftermath of the fire, citizens were concerned with saving what they could. One survivor recounted that on the night of the fire, many city residents slept in the streets, "whilst others, more fortunate in saving portions of their furniture, were compelled to watch it during the night, as the numerous thieves would otherwise have deprived them of what the element had spared."

The morning light revealed the extent of the losses. Many of Pittsburgh's founding buildings had been lost: the Custom House, the glass factory, several churches, and the mayor's office in Philo Hall were destroyed. The fire had devastated a twenty-four-block area, estimated at that time to represent two-thirds of the city's wealth. William Brackenridge, a guest at the fashionable Monongahela House hotel, wrote:

> The next morning I passed through the smoking ruins. So intense had been the heat that scarcely any appearance of wood was to be seen; even the ashes had disappeared. But for the smoke . . . it might have been taken for the ruins of some ancient city long since destroyed. . . . The reflection constantly uppermost with me was: Is there any hope that this ruin will be repaired? Can Pittsburgh ever recover from this blow?

The answer was yes. In fact, some have argued that the fire was actually a good thing for the city, in that it cleared away old structures and spurred new growth. Money for rebuilding efforts and relief funds poured in from around the country and the world. A new generation of factories secured the city's industrial strength. In his memoir, Judge Mellon wrote, "Instead of depression, [the fire] gave an impetus to every kind of business, especially everything in the building line. Mechanics of all kinds flocked in from other places, and all obtained ready employment at better wages than formerly; and new life and increased value was infused into real estate, and rents were higher for several years." Mellon himself was one of those benefiting from higher rents. In 1846, he built eighteen dwellings and reported a 10 percent return on his investment. He would go on to become the patriarch of the Mellon banking family—one of the richest in America.

The fire brought many changes to Pittsburgh, among them a greatly improved water system. The Monongahela Bridge destroyed in the blaze was replaced by the world's first suspension bridge, engineered by young John Roebling, who would later design the Brooklyn Bridge. The city's population doubled between 1840 and 1850, partially with an infusion of workers drawn by construction jobs. It would, however, be another twenty-five years before Pittsburgh would replace its volunteer fire units with a municipal department.

In 1945, on the one hundredth anniversary of the great fire, the Historical Society of Western Pennsylvania offered a $50 war bond to anyone who could prove the identity of the legendary washerwoman whose kettle fire ignited the great blaze. Many claimed to know who she was, but no one could provide conclusive proof, and her identity remains a mystery.

"THE TRAINS HAVE MET!"

The Camp Hill and Shohola Collisions
1856, 1864

The earliest days of America's railroad travel, in the 1830s and 1840s, were relatively safe. With locomotive technology in its infancy and few passenger lines running, accidents were rare. But that began to change in the 1850s, particularly in Pennsylvania, as the region pushed to supply the Industrial Revolution with coal and steel. Railroad traffic surged, bigger and stronger equipment rolled over improperly maintained tracks, and growing rail corporations struggled to hire competent engineers and station workers. Many of the runs between towns were on single tracks, with trains making use of occasional side spurs to pull off to let other trains pass. The telegraph was just beginning to be widely used, and most rail lines had no effective means of communicating between trains. These conditions came crashing together in two Pennsylvania rail collisions, less than a decade apart, that remain among the most dramatic in the country's history.

Camp Hill, July 17, 1856

The congregation of St. Michael's Roman Catholic Church in the Kensington section of Philadelphia rose early on the morning of Thursday, July 17, 1856. They had to be at the Master Street Depot by 5 A.M. and ready to leave onboard two trains that would take them to a church picnic in Fort Washington, 14 miles away. Mostly from hard-working Irish families, the church members were no doubt looking forward to a break from the summer heat of the city. But it took longer than expected to get 1,500 Sunday school children, teachers, and parents onboard the trains.

Still, Alfred Hoppel, the conductor of the first train, was confident he could make up the lost time. He knew this stretch of the North Penn lines well; his regular run was a passenger train heading south on the line from Gwynned. Though he had been alerted that a train was running that morning on the same single track, he did the math in his head and figured that after he made up some lost time, the trains could make use of a long siding at Edge Hill where they could safely pass one another.

At about 6 A.M., as the engineer of the southbound passenger train neared a blind curve near Camp Hill, he slowed his train and blew heavily on his whistle. The church excursion train, on a long downhill run and still trying to make up for lost time, gained speed and came around the blind curve with no time or way to avoid the approaching passenger train. The two locomotives collided head on, causing the boiler of the passenger train to explode in a blast that could be heard 5 miles away. The first three cars of the church excursion car were completely crushed, their wood providing fuel for a horrible fire.

A newspaper sketch depicted the chaotic collision of passenger and excursion trains near Camp Hill Station. FRANK LESLIE'S ILLUSTRATED WEEKLY, JULY 26, 1856

Fifty-nine people, most of them children, died in the crash and the flames that followed. The parish priest from St. Michael's also was killed. More than one hundred people were seriously injured, many with horrible burns.

The bodies of those killed were taken to a blacksmith shop, while the wounded were quickly carried to two nearby hotels and a boarding house. Many in the area rushed to help, with one newspaper account reporting, "Every woman who was not herself injured seemed to be attending to some wounded person, or mayhap watching a corpse. Every man or boy was willing to give way—to do all he could to relive [sic] the suffering which permeated the whole atmosphere." Another newspaper story relayed the following scene from one of the hotels:

A little, feeble infant was found in the ruins of one of the cars, piteously crying for its mother. No mother appeared to answer the summons. She was doubtlessly crushed to death. Quick as a thought, Mrs. G., one of the boarders at Bitting's Hotel, seized the little sufferer and placed it to her own breast, and there, under the burning rays of the sun, this woman, robbing, perhaps, her own infant of its nourishment, was sustaining this orphan, while all around was noise and confusion, and groans, and suffering, and death.

Throughout the day, a number of special trains made the run between the accident scene and Philadelphia. Those headed north carried panicked friends and family members; the southbound trains carried the injured and some of the charred bodies back to the Master Street Depot. Doctors onboard tried desperately to tend to the injured who were laid out on seats. A report printed in the *New York Daily Times* the following day recounted:

> The scene in the cars beggars description for horror. Every conceivable kind and degree of wound was to be seen, and nothing save signs of agony from the wounded, or their afflicted friends and relatives, met one's eyes at every turn. . . . When the trains reached the outer Depot, they were immediately beset by an anxious, earnest, tearful crowd of men, women and children, who pressed eagerly forward to the doors of the cars, and were kept back with great difficulty.

The scene at the accident site was equally as chaotic, as family members tried to find loved ones and tend to the wounded. A newspaper report described the scene: ". . . the fierce sun beat down upon the dead, the wounded, their rescuers and their half-crazed friends who were flocking to the scene, all running on foot, in wagons, and every species of vehicle that could be procured in the city. . . . As most of the victims were Irish, of course the demonstration of grief which met one's helpless ears were of the most violent character."

Newspapers also carried the report of a boy who had stayed behind while his mother and father went on the excursion. Upon hearing of the crash, the boy started out for the scene. He was picked up by a 5 P.M. train, exhausted and dehydrated, having walked almost 10 miles on foot.

By the end of the long day, most of the wounded had been returned to Philadelphia. As plans were made for a high mass to be said the next day at St. Michael's, calls went out for charity, with the president of the North Pennsylvania Railroad Company himself making a contribution of $500 to a fund for the victims' families.

William Vanstavoren, the conductor of the down train, was later to be cleared of all responsibility in the crash, but by then it was too late for him. Only slightly hurt in the collision, Vanstavoren stood by and watched as bodies were removed from the wreckage. He later hired a carriage to take him home, where that evening he swallowed a fatal dose of arsenic.

The coroner's jury that investigated the crash laid the blame at the feet of Alfred Hoppel, the conductor of the excursion train, for running the train on the track despite being behind schedule. He was arrested and charged with voluntary manslaughter, but was later acquitted, when the court ruled the railroad had no clear rules about running excursion trains on passenger tracks.

One of the heroes to emerge from the Camp Hill crash was a woman named Mary Johnson Ambler, a widowed mother of nine who lived nearby. Her home became a makeshift hospital, with neighbors using window shutters to carry the injured to her care. It was said that Mary Ambler worked tirelessly for hours, without stopping for food or water. Years later, when the town was looking for a new name for its rail station, it decided to honor Mary Ambler by naming the station after her, and two decades later, the entire community growing around the area was designated the Borough of Ambler.

Another lasting result from the Camp Hill crash was the introduction to America of railroad-inspired broadsides, large papers that up until that time had primarily dealt with political or social issues. Within weeks, broadsides memorializing the collision were being distributed. One, printed in Philadelphia by the J. H. Johnson Cheap Card and Job Printing Office, was titled "Verses on the Death of Miss Annie Lilly, One of the Victims of the Accident on the North Pennsylvania Railroad." It read in part:

Kind reader, view this happy throng
Of Merry children, bright and gay
With teachers, parents, tender friends
Start to enjoy a holiday.

Their merry faces seem to say
The city has no power to-day.
But with our swings, our hoops, our play,
We'll spend a glorious holiday.
And mid the laugh, the jest, the song,
The whistle sounds, the train moves on.

But oh! What means this sudden jar?
This wild confusion in the cars.
These shrieks that now assail the ear,
And fill the stoutest hearts with fear!
What flames are those, that now arise!
Those dying prayers, I'll ne'er forget,
"Have mercy, God!" The trains have met!

Shohola, July 15, 1864

The conditions were the same, the results just as horrific, but the circumstances entirely differently almost exactly eight years to the day in the northeastern corner of Pennsylvania, where the train tracks hug the curves of the Delaware River. By the summer of 1864, three years into the Civil War, northern prisons were running out of room for captured Confederates. The Union Army had just opened a new military prison in Elmira, New York, which by the end of the summer would hold nearly 10,000 prisoners. Some were being transferred from a facility in Point Lookout, Maryland, where they were moved by boat to Jersey City, then onto the Erie Railroad for the 275-mile leg to Elmira.

Early in the morning on July 15, two trains jammed with prisoners and guards were scheduled to make the journey; the first displayed special flags that signified a "second section" was following—a warning to railroaders along the way to keep the tracks clear until the second train had passed. But the second train was delayed an hour leaving Jersey City while guards tracked down several prisoners who had tried to make a break. The second train finally got underway at about 6 A.M. Onboard its seventeen cars were 833 Confederate prisoners and 128 Union guards. An added delay for a drawbridge opening brought the train into Port Jervis, New York, on the Pennsylvania border, four hours behind its lead train. At Port Jervis, the wood-burning train filled up with a fresh supply of fuel, and headed west onto its next leg, where the route switched to a single track. Engineer William Ingram spurred the locomotive on while fireman Daniel Tuttle fed wood into the furnace.

Heading east just over 20 miles away was a fifty-car coal train, pulled by a 38-ton engine. The coal train pulled into Lackawaxen, Pennsylvania, at about 2:30 P.M.; the junction at Lackawaxen had a rail spur where trains could clear the tracks for oncoming traffic. John Martin, the train's conductor, headed to the operator's station to make sure conditions were safe for him to proceed. Douglas "Duff" Kent was on duty. He gave Martin the all-clear to proceed, straight into the path of the oncoming train. (Investigators would later learn that Kent had been drinking heavily at a dance the night before and find him negligent in the crash. By that time, however, Kent had long disappeared.)

The section of track between Lackawaxen and Port Jervis clings to the shore of the Delaware River, around sharp curves and through deep hills. It was in one of these ravines—known as King and Fuller's Cut—that the two trains collided. They had no more than 100 yards to realize what was about to happen. Samuel Hoitt, the engineer of the coal train, had just enough time to leap from the engine before the crash, which shook the surrounding land and brought farmers running from their fields.

A *New York Tribune* report the following day recorded the scene: "The tender of the [Union train] was heaved upon end hurling its load of wood into the cab, effectually walling in both engineer and fireman against the hot boiler, and crushing them terribly. Both were found standing at their post, dead." The impact caused the wooden cars of the prisoner train to telescope into one another; of the 37 men traveling in the first car, 36 were killed instantly; the lone survivor was thrown clear of the wreckage. All told, at least 51 Confederate prisoners and 17 Union guards died either immediately or within several days of the disaster. More than 100 more were seriously injured.

The recollections of Frank Evans, one of the Union guards who survived, were recorded in a book about Sullivan County in the Civil War: ". . . the train came to a stop with a suddenness that hurled me to the ground, and instantly a crash arose, that rivaled the shock of battle, [and] filled that quiet valley. This lasted a moment. It was followed by a second or two of awful silence, and then the air was filled by the most appalling shrieks and wails and cries of anguish." Evans recounted hurrying forward on the train and seeing one of the guards perched on the reared-up end of the tender, dead, still with his gun in his hands.

Frantic rescue efforts began immediately. Guards and prisoners alike tore through the wreckage with their bare hands to rescue the injured. Residents of Shohola and other neighboring towns mobilized quickly to tend to the injured, using their wagons to carry the wounded to the train station in Shohola, where they were cared for in the freight and passenger rooms and on the platform. Two relief trains with supplies and doctors were dispatched, and physicians worked through the night. The *New York Times* reporter wrote, "The citizens of Shohola and Barreville (a village just across the Delaware) were untiring in their efforts to alleviate the sufferings of the wounded. Men, women and children vied with each other in acts of kindness." Those arriving at the scene were met by appalling conditions. The bodies of the dead from the first car had been carried to an embankment, most maimed beyond recognition. A second group of bodies was arranged in orderly rows beside the wreckage, while toward the rear of the train, the bodies of those guards who were killed were laid out in a field of rye. As described in a newspaper account, "Viewed by moonlight, and with lantern, it was a ghastly and horrible sight, although kindly hands had done much, by coverings of leaves, &c., to relieve the horror of the scene and the ghastliness of the dead."

A number of the uninjured Union guards quickly formed a circle around the disaster scene to prevent any uninjured prisoners from trying to escape, though it is believed that five Confederate soldiers did.

County officials decided to bury the dead beside the track without delay. Surviving prisoners and railroaders were put to work digging a 76-foot-long trench between the tracks and the river, while others used wood from the train cars to hammer together rough coffins. Four Confederates were placed into each coffin; around midnight, a shipment of pine boxes arrived, and each of the dead Union guards was given his own coffin. Though some later criticized the mass burial, those on the scene said that sanitary conditions required quick action and that although they did their best to identify the dead, the condition of some of the bodies made the task impossible.

Whatever wooden markers were placed identifying the graves rotted away over the years, and it wasn't until almost fifty years later that a farmer who had helped in the rescue pointed out the grave site. In 1911, the U.S. government determined that the bodies should be moved to the Woodlawn National Cemetery at Elmira, where they were once again laid in a mass grave. A stone monument marks the spot, with the names of the Confederate soldiers listed on a bronze plaque on the southern side, and the names of the Union soldiers facing north.

"A ROAR LIKE THUNDER"

The Johnstown Flood
1889

It had been raining heavily since the day before, but the clouds let up just long enough for the citizens of Johnstown, Pennsylvania, to hold their Memorial Day parade on May 30, 1889. Indeed, the town had much to celebrate. It was a thriving industrial community, its population spurred in the 1850s by the arrival of the Pennsylvania Railroad and the Cambria Iron Company. Thirty thousand people now called Johnstown home, and the town was greatly admired for the quality of its steel.

There was a drawback to life here, however. The town had been built on a floodplain at the convergence of the Little Conemaugh and Stony Creek Rivers, and springtime thaws made flooding commonplace. Residents were accustomed to slogging through muddy streets and moving belongings to higher ground when the spring rains came. The benefits of life in the booming town made the inconvenience bearable.

Fourteen miles upstream, life was even better for members of the South Fork Fishing and Hunting Club. Prosperous families from Pittsburgh had built summer retreats around a large, 450-acre man-made lake; membership rosters included such wealthy industrial magnates as Andrew Mellon, Andrew Carnegie, and Henry Clay Frick. The club had purchased the land in 1879, made repairs to an abandoned railroad dam, and raised the level of the lake for their fishing pleasure. Members kept a cautious eye on the dam, with annual jokes about whether it would hold for another spring thaw. There had been a dam break back in 1862, but that was before the club made its repairs, and year after year the dam held, so few worried about it. Daniel Morrell, the president of Johnstown's Cambria Iron Company, had made a formal request to the club to strengthen the dam; he was assured, "You and your people are in no danger from our enterprise."

But 1889 was not a normal year. Heavy snowfalls during the late winter and early spring had left the ground saturated, and April and May had both seen heavier-than-normal rainfalls. On May 28, a storm moved out of Kansas and Nebraska, and every town along the storm's path reported extremely heavy rain. On the morning of May 30, the U.S. Signal Service issued a warning to the mid-Atlantic states: Threatening weather was on its way. Some streets in Johnstown were already under water, and several bridges in the area had been washed out; train traffic was backing up because of track washouts and mudslides. Some families in Johnstown had begun to move their belongings to higher ground, and some had left their homes altogether, seeking shelter in drier buildings and the homes of friends.

By the morning of May 31, Elias Unger was worried. President of the South Fork Fishing and Hunting Club, it was his job to keep an eye on the dam, and he discovered that water levels in the lake had risen more than 2 feet from the night before. Unger put crews to work shoring up the dam. They began digging a new spillway for water runoff and clearing debris blocking existing drainage. Others worked trying to make the dam taller.

But at 3:10 P.M., the dam gave way. One man who had been keeping a wary eye on the repair work said that the break started slowly. "It run over a short spell," he recalled, "and then about half of the roadway just fell down over the dam. And then it just cut through like a knife." The lake released its 20 million tons of water with a force later compared to that of Niagara Falls. It took just forty-five minutes for the lake to totally empty its contents into the valley below. Elias Unger would later say, ". . . it seemed to me as if all the destructive elements of the Creator had been turned loose at once in that awful current of water."

Two miles downstream of the club lay the small town of South Fork. There the waters destroyed several dozen homes and killed coal miner Michael Mann—the first victim of the flood. His body wasn't found until a week later, more than a mile downstream. Just past South Fork, the valley narrowed considerably, increasing the force of the water and pushing it as high as 75 feet. And by this time, the surging waters had already picked up large pieces of trees, railroad ties, and dislodged track. The rush of water and debris ran into a 71-foot-high railroad viaduct, which held for several minutes, then collapsed under the pressure.

The flood then set its sights on Mineral Point, a town a mile below the viaduct. Witnesses described how by this point the water was ripping trees out by the roots and stripping hillsides down to bare rock. In Mineral Point, houses were ripped from their foundations, and railroad locomotives were washed

Ruins of a viaduct bridge. LIBRARY OF CONGRESS, LC-USZ62-94718

along by the growing wave of water and debris. The town was destroyed.

Describing the water plowing onward toward the town of East Conemaugh, one resident said it looked like "a huge hill rolling over and over." The noise level was growing as well, as the crushing sounds of the debris added to the roar of the water. In the railroad yards outside of East Conemaugh, an engineer named John Hess heard the roar and figured out what was coming. Tying down the whistle of his train, he sped toward town blasting a loud whistle of warning. Though Hess is credited with saving many lives, fifty people in East Conemaugh died, including twenty-five who were stranded on trains. Lou Dallmyer, a passenger who escaped, would later recount, "Many of the passengers in their mad, frantic efforts to release themselves dashed their hands and faces against the windows, the broken glass cutting gashes from which the blood flowed in streams. Some of the men succeeded in climbing to the tops of cars, only to be dashed off into the water when the former would strike against some obstacle." The railroad station was destroyed, and witnesses watched in horror as the waters took fifty-ton locomotives and continued on their way.

The next town of Woodvale, a community developed by the Cambria Iron Company, had no warning. Within ten minutes, the town was gone. More than 300 people, a third of Woodvale's population, died that day. The town had also been home to the Gautier Wire Works, which exploded and added miles of barbed wire to the wall of debris headed straight for Johnstown. The weight of the debris carried along on the top of the water created additional force, causing the wave, still some 40 feet high, to continually roll over on itself with a crushing ferocity.

At 4:07 P.M., that wave plowed into Johnstown, preceded by a combination of dirt, smoke, and steam that some would later call a "death mist." A deafening sound of crashing water and debris that some described as a "roar like thunder" was accompanied by factory whistles and church bells sounding warning calls. One man said "the water coming looked like a cloud of the blackest smoke I ever saw." It took just ten minutes for the water to totally inundate the town, as panicked residents tried to grab their children and struggle to higher ground. An observer watching from a nearby hillside said the streets of the town "grew black with people running for their lives."

As the water slammed into Johnstown, it split into several torrents, one plowing through the existing river channel and another headed straight for the downtown area. In its way

Debris at the warehouse of Cambria Iron Works. LIBRARY OF CONGRESS, LC-USZ62-315

stood the Methodist church on Franklin Street, which was heavily damaged, but still stands to this day. By taking the brunt of the wave, the church saved several buildings behind it, including Alma Hall, the tallest building in Johnstown at the time, which would become the surviving shelter for 264 people that evening. (One survivor, James Walter, claimed that he was washed out of his home on Walnut Street onto a floating roof, then thrown through a window into his own office in Alma Hall, where he weathered the night.) Alma Hall remains a Johnstown landmark today.

Much of the rest of Johnstown, however, was destroyed. Houses and buildings were wiped out, and the desperate struggle to survive began. Those who could scrambled to higher ground in hopes of finding safety, while others clung to whatever they could hold on to. Many were trapped in the water. One survivor remembered, "I kept paddling and grabbing and spitting and spitting and trying to keep the sticks and dirt and this horrible water out of my mouth." Houses, some with dozens of people clinging to the roofs, floated along with the rushing water. While the churning debris crushed some, it yielded wood that for others became life-saving rafts.

For a sixteen-year-old named Victor Heiser, a roof floating by became a door to his future. Heiser was in his family's barn that day when he saw his father gesturing wildly toward the roof. Heiser climbed to the roof of the barn in time to watch his family's home be swept away in the wave of water. Heiser too was carried away, but managed to leap onto the roof of a passing brick house. He spent the night there in the attic with nineteen other people and was the only survivor in his family. (Heiser would go on to become an acclaimed doctor; his development of the first effective treatment of leprosy was credited with saving as many as two million lives.)

Families fled to attics, and those in buildings downtown raced up flights of stairs ahead of the water, which reached as high as the third story in some buildings. The pastor of the Franklin Street Methodist Church, Reverend H. L. Chapman, was at his home when the wave hit. He reported opening his front door only to see a railroad car float past with a man clinging on. Yelling for his family to head for the attic, Reverend Chapman thought to turn off the gas fire. As he passed the front door, it gave way, and the floodwaters rushed in. Chapman was able to climb to the attic, where he and his family spent an anxious hour listening to the waters rush through their house below. Though the porch was ripped off and much of his furniture destroyed, Chapman would later write, "I think none of us was afraid to meet God, but all felt willing to put it off until a more propitious time."

In just ten minutes, it was over. The waters rushed through town on to the Pennsylvania Railroad's Stone Bridge below Johnstown. This barrier finally held, but its strength resulted in a huge logjam that reached up to 40 feet in some places. Piled up at the bridge in a mass of oily water were thousands of tons of debris, including building material and machines, many railroad cars and miles of track, sections of bridges that collapsed upstream, along with trees, animals, and—worst of all—hundreds of people struggling to survive and the bodies of those who had not. Some became entangled in the miles of barbed wire that washed away from the Gautier Wire Works. It was estimated that the mass of debris held back by the bridge covered more than thirty acres.

As darkness surrounded Johnstown, frantic rescue efforts continued. Those left huddling in attics or on rooftops still had to contend with huge currents battering the buildings; indeed, many buildings collapsed even after the initial onslaught was over. The untenable situation grew even more dire during the evening when the oily debris at the bridge caught fire, turning the debris field into a raging fire that one Johnstown newspaper described as burning with "all the fury of hell." It is estimated that eighty people who survived the floodwaters lost their lives in the fire that followed. The blaze blanketed the area with acrid smoke, but it also provided the only light that shone in Johnstown that night. W. Horace Rose, a prominent Johnstown citizen, would later write his recollections of that night: "I shall not attempt to describe the terrors of the following night, with its thousand and one alarms, as the crash of buildings was heard as they settled in the water or were crushed by the weight

This stereograph image was entitled "The Johnstown Calamity:
A slightly damaged house." LIBRARY OF CONGRESS, LC-USZ62-46831

from above. Suffice it to say, it was a night of awful terror, and over all was the ghastly and lurid light that came from the burning debris at the stone bridge below."

It would be months, even years, before the complete scope of the tragedy was known. Bodies of presumed flood victims were discovered as late as 1911, one as far as 600 miles away in Cincinnati. In total, 2,209 people lost their lives. Ninety-nine entire families were wiped out; 396 children were killed, and more than 300 men and women were left widowed. Four square miles of downtown Johnstown were obliterated, and 1,600 homes destroyed, with an estimated property damage of 17 million 1889 dollars.

Among the most poignant stories from the flood was that of the Fenn family. As the flood approached, John Fenn left his wife, Anna, at home to help a neighbor move furniture to higher ground. He was washed away when the wall of water slammed down, leaving Anna home with seven children. Struggling to hold her young baby above the floodwaters while her six other children clung to her, Anna Fenn was forced to watch all of her children drown. "The water rose and floated us until our heads nearly touched the ceiling," she later recounted. "It was dark and the house was tossing every way. The air was stifling, and I could not tell just the moment the rest of the children had to give up and drown . . . What I suffered, with the bodies of my seven children floating around me in the gloom can never be told." Anna Fenn was rescued fifteen hours later from a roof of a house downstream. She gave birth to a baby girl a few weeks after the flood, but that child did not survive either. Anna eventually remarried and moved to Virginia. She is buried in Johnstown's Grandview Cemetery, where a large monument marks her grave.

Club House Press, looking south. LIBRARY OF CONGRESS, LC-USZ62-79333

It is said that as day broke there was an eerie silence hanging over Johnstown. Overnight, the waters had receded, leaving behind streets clogged with mud and debris. About the
scene that met survivors the following morning, David Beale
would write, "It were vain to undertake to tell the world how or
what we felt, when shoeless, hatless, and many of us almost

naked, some bruised and broken, we stood there and looked upon that scene of death and desolation." Several fires continued to burn and smoldered for days. The threat of disease became an immediate concern, and ultimately typhoid would claim forty additional victims.

Word of the disaster spread quickly, and hundreds of rescue workers and journalists flocked to the city. The first relief train arrived from Pittsburgh on the morning of June 1. A fire crew onboard is credited with dousing the flames at the Stone Bridge, which many were calling a funeral pyre. Among the first crews from Pittsburgh were fifty-five undertakers, who set about organizing temporary morgues.

Graphic photographs and the accounts of reporters prompted a huge outpouring of good will around the country, though the reports were not known for their accuracy or journalistic restraint. A June 3 account in a Philadelphia newspaper related the following:

> And now above the roar of the waters agonizing cries went up to Heaven for salvation. Can anyone imagine it? No description that would be penned could even begin to touch upon the horrors of that expiring day and night. . . . Whole families were floated off together. . . . Husbands were parted from wives, children from mothers and fathers. Parents were drowned before their children's eyes, children before their parents. In a few moments Johnstown, buried under water, was a vast sea upon which floated and tossed the wrecks of hundreds and hundreds of houses.

Money, clothing, and food poured into Johnstown, and the relief effort from the United States and eighteen foreign countries would grow to $3.7 million. (Among those donating money to the effort were Andrew Carnegie and other members of the South Fork Fishing and Hunting Club.) Rescue workers organized emergency hospitals while others set about caring for the 25,000 survivors who needed food, clothing, and housing.

Leading the charge was the newly formed American Red Cross in its first major peacetime relief effort. Founder Clara Barton and a Red Cross crew arrived in Johnstown on June 5, and Barton would remain there through the end of October, helping to distribute supplies to thousands of survivors. She oversaw the building of "Red Cross hotels" to house merchants and businessmen. The Philadelphia Red Cross, a separate organization, also hurried to town and set up a medical relief center at the Cambria Iron Company. When Barton left Johnstown, the citizens came together and presented her with a diamond locket as a thank-you gift for her efforts.

Pennsylvania Governor James Beaver called out the militia to help restore order to the town. Within days there were 10,000 men working on the cleanup and recovery. It took just fourteen days for the Pennsylvania Railroad to rebuild 20 miles of track and bridges, reopening its route to the East. On June 9, the Cambria Iron Works announced that it would rebuild in Johnstown and within six weeks, huge piles of wreckage had been removed and the town was beginning to rebuild. By July 1, several stores on Main Street had reopened, and the town even managed to organize a small Independence Day celebration on July 4.

Anger and the finger of blame soon fell on the South Fork Fishing and Hunting Club for failing to properly maintain its dam. One Harrisburg newspaper ran an editorial saying, "Fifty thousand lives in Pennsylvania were jeopardized for eight years that a club of rich pleasure seekers might fish and sail and revel in luxurious ease during the heated term." Numerous damage suits were filed against the club, but the courts ultimately ruled that the collapse of the dam was an "act of God." No flood survivors received any compensation.

Despite the scope of the tragedy, Pennsylvania did not pass a state dam-inspection law until 1913, and then, only after a dam collapse in the town of Austin killed seventy-eight people. Johnstown continued to suffer flooding in the spring, but nothing ever came close to the flood of 1889. Still, severe flooding in 1936 prompted the Flood Control Act of 1936, and the Army Corps of Engineers completed the Johnstown Local Flood Protection Program, a series of channel improvements in the area, in 1943. A 1977 flood left seven counties around Johnstown declared disaster areas and killed eighty people, though officials credited the flood protection program with preventing a far worse tragedy.

On May 31, 1892—the three-year anniversary of the flood—10,000 people gathered at Johnstown's Grandview Cemetery for the unveiling of what was called the Monument to the Unknown Dead. Behind the monument stretch the graves of 750 flood victims who were never identified. In an editorial the next day, a local newspaper stated, "It may be well to consider that the flood, with its train of horrors, is behind us, and that we have henceforth to do with the future alone."

DISASTER UNDERGROUND

Coal Mine Calamities
1904, 1907, 1908

Coal mining has long been a cornerstone of industry in Pennsylvania. The discovery of "black diamonds" in the hills of the state helped fuel the Industrial Revolution, offering an economical fuel alternative to the dwindling supplies of wood and charcoal. Transportation networks sprung up to move the coal throughout the country, and mining provided jobs to hundreds of thousands of immigrants looking to start new lives in the United States.

But danger is a bedrock of the coal miner's life. The process of mining, breaking, and loading tons of coal is difficult and dangerous. After a series of horrible disasters in the nineteenth century, mine workers began to organize and fight for improved conditions and safety in the mines. Labor advocate Mother Jones began working with Pennsylvania coal miners in the 1890s, and for eight months in 1902, 150,000 workers went on strike, staying out of the mines to protest working conditions. Though not all of their conditions were met, the sense was that things were getting safer in the mines. Or so everyone thought.

Harwick Mine, Cheswick, January 25, 1904

The early morning inspector had given the all-clear for the miners at the Allegheny Coal Company's Harwick Mine near Pittsburgh to begin work at about 6 A.M. on January 25, 1904. Several cars loaded with coal had already been sent to the surface. Shortly after 8 A.M., a signal from the bottom of the shaft indicated another car was ready to come up, so a cage with a mule onboard was sent down into the mine.

Just as it hit the ground, something went horribly wrong. A huge explosion sent the cage hurtling back up the shaft through the roof of the tipple where the cars were emptied, trapping the miners underground. The nearby weighmaster's office was destroyed, and the body of the mule was later found 200 feet away. Two workers manning the tipple died a short time later. The airshaft was also damaged in the explosion, and it was two hours before workers could begin pumping fresh air into the mine. Desperate rescue attempts began as soon as it was safe, which included crews from nearby mines that were sent to the scene of the explosion. Someone counted the number of lamps that had been taken into the mines that morning so they would have some idea how many men they were searching for. The answer was discouraging: 184.

The first person to head down the shaft was James McCann. He tried to get down through the air shaft, but found it blocked, and it was not until late afternoon that McCann was lowered down the main shaft. There he found sixteen-year-old Adolph Gunia, horribly burned, and immediately brought him up to the surface. "I was working about 240 feet from the main shaft when suddenly the air became very cold," Gunia would later recall. "I thought I would freeze . . . The cold air was immediately followed by blinding light. Then I knew no more."

At a makeshift morgue, friends and relatives identify remains of the explosion's 180 victims, some as young as fifteen. PHOTO COURTESY ALLEGHENY KISKI VALLEY HISTORICAL SOCIETY, TARENTUM, PA.

Other rescuers descended into the mine, some being turned back by blocked passageways or because they were overcome by fumes. One of the first people lowered down was Selwyn Taylor. Well known in the mining world, Taylor was the engineer who had plotted the Harwick mine. Along with him was Thomas Wood, who said later, "Taylor laid out the mine and seemed to know the way. . . . We passed the third, fourth, and fifth heading and then through an overdraft into the airshaft. I began to feel dizzy and sick, and then I saw Taylor stagger and fall." A mine inspector was lowered down and found Taylor's body soon thereafter.

As word of the explosion spread, friends and family hurried to the mine for word of their loved ones. A reporter on the scene wrote, "The scene about the mouth of the pit was pitiful. Hundreds of wives and children surrounded the mouth of the shaft crazed with grief and anxiously awaiting any news from the entombed men."

The next day, coal miner Daniel Lyle traveled 15 miles from his home to help in the rescue efforts. Lyle and two other men entered the mine, working late into the evening. Though the two other men surfaced the next morning, Lyle was overcome by gases. His body was found later well inside the mine.

Rescue attempts continued for two days despite bitter winter weather conditions, but there were no more rescues. One hundred and eighty miners died in the Harwick mine explosion. Adolph Gunia was the only survivor. Inspectors would later say the blast was caused by a spark igniting methane gas that had built up in the mine. The air shaft had been coated with ice, reducing the ventilation of fresh air from the surface.

Upon learning that two men had died during the rescue attempt, Pittsburgh steelmaker Andrew Carnegie offered $5 million to establish the Carnegie Hero Fund, charged with honoring "civilization's heroes" who risk their lives to save others. Since its founding, the Fund has awarded nearly 9,000 medals and distributed more than $28 million to recipients.

Darr Mine, Jacobs Creek, December 19, 1907

Ventilation problems were also to blame for an explosion about three years later not far away, at the Pittsburgh Coal Company's Darr Mine in Jacobs Creek. December 1907 had been a horrible month for the mining industry. Just two weeks earlier in Monongah, West Virginia, 361 miners were killed in a disaster that remains this country's worst. Surely that tragedy was on the minds of workers at the Darr Mine, where some had long complained about the air quality.

A mine foreman had gotten the company to agree to dig a new ventilation shaft, and workers had just 40 feet to go to connect the shaft with the existing tunnel. Yet at about 11:30 A.M. on December 19, the earth shook for miles around the mine, and there was little doubt about what had happened. One newspaper account stated, "There was but one explosion and it was accompanied by a flaming detonation. While the surface indications do not show that it came with great force, residents of both sides of the [Youghiogheny] river say that their houses shook and the earth fairly rumbled as the gas and dust made a fruitless effort to belch itself forth through any entrance."

Rescue crews converged at the mine. A local newspaper described their efforts: "With all the sadness that the accident took on, in the same ratio of sobriety was the work of rescue begun. Men seemed to fairly spring from the ground, anxious to pull down the barriers between their unfortunate fellowmen and liberty, which in this case meant life." But it soon became apparent that no one could have survived the blast. The total number of dead was placed at 239, many of them Hungarian immigrants. The death toll could have been far worse, however. An estimated 200 miners had taken the day off to celebrate St. Nicholas Day at local churches.

It took several days to recover all of the bodies. The U.S. government stepped in to handle the recovery efforts, aided by a then-new, self-contained breathing device for use in deep-mine rescues. Investigators would later say that the explosion was caused by a group of miners who had entered a cordoned-

off area carrying open lamps. After the explosion, the Pittsburgh Coal Company prohibited open lamps in its mines. The
company purchased a plot of land in nearby Smithton, where
many of the miners are buried.

As a result of the disasters at the Darr and Monongah
mines, the U.S. Geological Survey created a Mine Accidents
Division and began to work on ways to improve mine rescue
techniques. The following year, the number of mining deaths
began to decline, and 1907 would go down as the worst year in
mining history.

Marianna Mine, Marianna, November 28, 1908

The Pittsburgh–Buffalo Coal Company's mine at Marianna
was supposed to be a model of safety and improved working
and living conditions for miners. Constructed in 1907, the
community boasted brick houses with indoor plumbing; the
company's president had traveled to Europe to research safe
mine designs. The facility was impressive enough that on
October 14, 1908, President Theodore Roosevelt traveled to
Marianna to tour the new plant. But just forty-four days later,
on November 28, the Marianna mine was rocked by a terrible
explosion.

Just as a mine inspector was emerging from the shaft, having declared conditions underground safe, a blast shook one of
the mines in the three-mine complex, destroying the ventilation shaft servicing all the mining areas. A cage carrying one
miner crashed back down its shaft, blocking access to that
entrance. Rescue crews soon arrived at the scene, as did John
H. Jones, president of Pittsburg–Buffalo. A newspaper report
the following day recorded the scene:

Wrecked tipple at the Marianna mine disaster. LIBRARY OF CONGRESS, LC-B2-619-4

President Jones, with his overcoat, gum boots, miner's cap and gloves soon descended the shaft accompanied by the superintendent. . . . This man who knows mining as no other man in the Pittsburgh district, who knows his mines and who has faith in this great masterpiece appeared strong and brave. He was. There was no faint heart in his bosom, no unsteady nerves, no shaking footsteps. But he must have known ere he started down this dark shaft to the great tunnel below that his men were not alive. When he came back he looked sorrowful—for the situation was clear to him then. The men were dead—they could not have possibly lived.

One hundred fifty-four miners lost their lives in the explosion. It would be several days before all of their bodies could be retrieved. One of the victims was a nephew of Jones; he was on his first day back at work following his honeymoon.

The only happiness that day in Marianna occurred late in the evening. "About 10 o'clock to-night a shout was heard at the mouth of the shaft that there was a living man below," the *New York Times* reported the following day. "Then there was a rushing for the safety helmets, and with these and a stretcher a rescuing party was lowered away in the bucket, buckling on the helmets as they descended."

The lone survivor was a German immigrant, Fred Elinger, whose body and eyes had been badly burned. In broken English, Elinger told reporters what he remembered.

> I was working at laying brick in one of the entries and the first thing I knew a terrible explosion took place, which threw me some distance. My two buddies were also tossed some distance away. I heard them for a while and then all was quiet. I was overcome by the afterdamp and fell asleep. I do not know how long I slept, but when I awoke I started at once for my dinner pail. It could not be found and then I started to hunt for the air shaft as I knew I had been working near it. I moped about in the mines for some time and heard the rescuers at work nearby, I thought they were going back without finding me and I at once yelled as best I could and then they came.

A writer for the local paper reported thusly:

> The calamity has cast a gloom over the entire community for miles around and contributions are being made, the money

The dead being carried out of the Marianna mine on stretchers.
LIBRARY OF CONGRESS, LC-B2-618-15

to go toward aiding the widows and children who were left practically penniless and without a means of livelihood, by the sudden taking away of the ones who furnished their bread and butter. Thanksgiving, the miners did not work, spending the day with their families and friends. All was gayness; the next day suffering and death.

There was a mass burial of the Marianna miners at the nearby Scenery Hill Cemetery, though many bodies could not be identified, and the remains of some victims were never found.

Though the safety of coal mining improved dramatically in the years that followed, the industry remains one of the world's most dangerous. As one reporter at the scene of the Harwick explosion wrote, "The history of Pennsylvania is full of such disasters, alike in most of the details and in the heartrending scenes about the pit's mouth."

"A PERFECT HELL"

Harrisburg Rail Yard Explosion

1905

It was quite an impressive list of passengers on the Cleveland and Cincinnati Express that pulled out of Philadelphia at 11:05 P.M. on May 10, 1905. Onboard were several respected citizens: the wife of the publisher of one of Pittsburgh's major newspaper, the daughter of a U.S. senator, the son-in-law of a Pennsylvania Railroad executive, and several millionaires from Pittsburgh's business community. Sam Shubert, the renowned New York theatrical producer, was also on the train. Most of those onboard quickly got into their nightclothes and settled down for the overnight trip across the state.

Two hours later, near Harrisburg, a sixty-eight-car freight train was heading east, entering the rail yards in the Lochiel neighborhood on the city's south side. The engineer of the freighter pulled the air brakes when he saw a switcher on the tracks ahead, screeching to a halt in time to avoid a collision. But the quick stop caused a boxcar thirty-four cars back to buckle and list into the westbound tracks, just as the ten-car express out of Philadelphia was speeding in from the east at 60 miles per hour. That boxcar was packed with ten tons of explosive blasting powder made partially of dynamite.

There was no time to stop the passenger train. Robert Dickey, a fireman, was the only person onboard who actually saw what happened. "We saw that the freight train had buckled . . . and some of the cars began to topple over toward our track," he said later. "Thomas, the engineer, knew that the only chance of safety was to get by before any of the cars struck ours. He let the engine out another notch, and she sped by the tilting cars." The engine, the baggage car, the smoker, and the day coach made it by. But the first Pullman car, named Socrates, sideswiped the tilting boxcar, setting off a disastrous chain reaction. "That's all I know," Dickey would say. "When I woke up I was laying on the grass by the river bank with an awful pain in my back."

First one explosion, then another and another rocked the rail yard and were felt for miles around. The Socrates was incinerated, then the flames spread to the six Pullman cars behind. George Hayes, a brakeman onboard the express, would later tell a Harrisburg newspaper, "Everything outside was red with flames. It seemed like a perfect hell."

Some passengers were thrown from the exploding cars, and a few ended up in the nearby Susquehanna River. They were among the lucky ones. The rest fought to escape from the burning train, while still more explosions went off around them. A reporter for the *Philadelphia Inquirer* wrote the next day, "Men of millions, women of the highest social rank fought for life amid that frightful scene. Naked and shrieking from agonizing burns, the passengers pulled themselves from amid the heaps of twisted iron and splintered wood, or found them-

View of the Pennsylvania Railroad wreck at Harrisburg, May 11, 1905.
INSTITUTE OF AMERICAN DELTIOLOGY, MYERSTOWN, PA.

selves held fast while the flames came slowly nearer and nearer until their last cry was smothered amid the smoke."

Many of the early reports from the scene were equally as horrifying. The initial dispatch to the *New York Times* that appeared that morning, estimated that at least 163 people were believed killed, stating, "Many of the people on the train were blown to atoms and no trace of them will ever be found." Mercifully, that report turned out to be greatly exaggerated. The death toll released the following day was twenty-three, although there were reports that several others died later of their burns. The bodies of some victims were so badly burned that they were identifiable only by the jewelry they had been wearing. More than one hundred people were seriously injured by burns or in their desperate attempts to escape.

Harvey Feldman and his wife were in a sleeper car on their way home from New York to Franklin, Pennsylvania. "We were sleeping soundly when all at once came the slight explosion that partly awoke us," he told a Philadelphia reporter at the scene. "This was followed by the most awful roar I ever heard, and in an instant we were dashed against the side of the car. We groped around in the dark and finally got out of the window, losing everything. . . . We had to walk over the sharp cinders in our bare feet and they are badly cut."

People living nearby heard the explosions—windows were blown out in the nearest homes—and firefighters and rescuers were on the scene right away. While some firemen struggled in the dark to locate fireplugs, others took off their coats and gave them to victims, most of who were in their nightclothes. According to the account in the *Philadelphia Inquirer*, "Out of the entire list of passengers not more than a score were clothed when they found themselves launched into the night. Women begged for the slightest means of protection and the men did all in their power to provide for the greater sufferers." Neighbors also pitched in, providing blankets, and some passengers who had thought to grab their suitcases distributed the contents to those in need. The railroad company eventually got two nearby clothing stores to open so the passengers could be provided with clothes. Other neighbors offered their carts and automobiles to transport the wounded to the hospital.

In all, there were ten separate explosions counted by some of the survivors. Charles Rosenstock, a traveling salesman from New York, related his experience to the *New York Times* upon his return to Manhattan, saying he was hurled from his berth and escaped through a window with only a torn night robe. "I ran along the track for some distance when a second explosion occurred. It lifted me off my feet and blew me a hundred feet through the air. I went clear over the embankment and landed on the edge of the river. There were other men and women there before me, and more came sailing through the air after me. The flames of the exploding dynamite were so noxious that I had to throw myself into the river to escape being suffocated." He was transported to Harrisburg Hospital, where he saw "sights so gruesome that they beggar description." There he eventually met a nearby resident who took Rosenstock to his home, gave him clothes, and handed him enough money to take a train back to New York. Survivors reported many similar stories of neighbors opening their homes to them.

Even the governor of Pennsylvania, Samuel Pennypacker, took in some of the train's passengers. A woman identified in newspaper reports only as Mrs. Tindel of Pittsburgh, daughter of Pennsylvania Senator P. C. Knox, and her husband walked away from the wreckage but were slightly injured by flying glass. They immediately placed a call to the governor, who sent his private secretary to the scene to retrieve Mr. and Mrs. Tindel and take them to the governor's mansion, where they received clothing and medical care.

Theater magnate Samuel Shubert was sleeping in the second-to-last Pullman car. In a separate berth in the car was Abe Thaleheimer, manager of the "Fantana" theater production, who was accompanying Shubert to Pittsburgh. "I was asleep when I was awakened by a terrific explosion," Mr. Thaleheimer told a *New York Times* reporter at the scene. "I crawled out of the window with nothing on but my pajamas. I made my way down the embankment at the side of the railroad, and then I thought of Sam. By the light of the burning cars I could see him pinned in his berth. Crawling up on a portion of the car which had been blown off, I managed to get at Mr. Shubert, and tried to arouse him to a sense of his danger."

According to Thaleheimer, Shubert said, "Go away and let me die." "I simply answered, 'Not today,' and pulled him out of the car," Thaleheimer continued. "In my bare feet I climbed down over the sharp stones of the embankment, again carrying Sam on my back." Shubert was badly burned below the waist and was rushed to the hospital for treatment. "In my anxiety for him I forgot that I was almost naked and covered with blood until I was reminded of that fact in the hospital," Thaleheimer said. Although it appeared at first that Shubert would survive, he died the following day. His body was carried back to New York in a special train car, where it was met by a large crowd of friends and family.

The raging fire in the rail yard burned through the night, with the flames providing the only light for rescuers and those giving medical care. Policeman H. C. Weirich was one of the first to reach the scene. He helped several victims crawl out of the windows before being driven back by the flames. He told a newspaper reporter, "Only by the light of the flames could we see to work, and every once in a while we could hear some unfortunate pinned in a burning car begging to be killed. It was awful, especially when you think that there were plenty of men there to take up the work of rescue, but were prevented from getting near the train by the intense heat."

There were numerous dramatic rescue stories that circulated after the disaster. Two women told a Philadelphia newspaper that they were trapped at one end of a Pullman car and couldn't get the door open. With flames creeping closer, a few sticks of dynamite that hadn't yet exploded burst the door open, allowing them to escape. One woman told a reporter that she owed her life to the fact that she was unable to secure a berth on the train when she was at the Philadelphia train station. She decided to take a seat in the day coach, which escaped most of the damage.

But the most amazing story of survival told in the newspapers was that of a four-month-old baby, traveling in the day coach with her mother. The mother said she had wrapped the sleeping child in a shawl and placed her on a package rack shortly before the explosion. According to a report the following day in the *New York Times,* "All was dark in this car, and the mother, thrown from the seat, fled wildly down the aisle . . . before she knew what was happening she was hurled from the car and fell along the rails. Her face was scratched by cinders and stone." According to the account, a man named J. M. Bamford, who lived nearby, dragged the hysterical woman away from the wreckage and down the river embankment. There they found her baby—uninjured—lying on a seat cushion 50 feet from the wreck, sucking her thumb. In the reporter's words, "The baby . . . had her eyes wide open and was kicking her feet as if the flames and the noise and the excitement had been got up for her especial benefit."

By the middle of the night, there were an estimated 1,000 railroad crewmen at the scene working to clear the tracks. Service was restored on the line the following day. Though the railroad was later cleared of all responsibility, the disaster shed light on the danger of moving explosives by rail. At the coroner's inquest, workers testified that dangerous materials were sometimes concealed from handlers, that freight cars carrying explosives were sometimes joined with passenger cars, and that explosives were frequently loosely packed in freight cars.

The U.S. Senate later passed a bill specifying strict regulations for packing and shipping explosives by rail.

The Pennsylvania Railroad paid to have the remains of unidentified victims buried at the nearby Paxtang Cemetery and erected a monument there with the names of all those killed in the disaster.

"LIGHTED IN A FLASH"

The Boyertown Opera House Fire
1908

As 1907 drew to a close, life was good in Boyertown, a small Pennsylvania Dutch town of about 2,000 nestled in the rolling hills of eastern Berks County. The editor of the local paper praised the advances the past year had brought—paved streets and a new gas plant. "In addition," wrote Charles B. Spatz in the December 28, 1907, edition of the *Berks County Democrat*, "about 50 new modern homes were built, half a dozen new streets were opened, many desirable citizens were added, the casket factory was considerably enlarged, the death rate small and the birth rate large . . . Let the march of progress continue." The town was considering installing electric streetlights in the coming months.

Spatz had every reason to be optimistic and excited about the new year. Not only was Boyertown booming, but he and other members of St. John's Lutheran Church were busy preparing for a special church-sponsored performance of "The Scottish Reformation," to be presented at the town's Rhoads

Opera House on January 13 and 14. This was to be no small-scale church pageant. The popular traveling show featured the latest slide projection technology and a dramatic staging with actors and church members in fancy costumes. Cast members had been practicing for weeks; organizers had even brought a professional in from Washington, D.C., to coach the cast. In total, more than sixty citizens of Boyertown were to be involved on stage.

Their relatives and friends were understandably eager to take in the production, and performances for both nights quickly sold out. On opening night, organizers arranged extra chairs along the sides of the auditorium to handle the 310 people who crowded in to see the show. That was just one of many avoidable conditions that led to the tragedy that followed—a devastating fire in which whatever could go wrong did.

The Rhoads Opera House had been built in 1885 by Dr. Thomas Rhoads, an admired Boyertown physician and founder of the Farmers National Bank, which occupied part of the building's first floor. A large auditorium took up most of the second floor, with the third floor given over to meeting space for the town's lodges and a dressing room to service the auditorium. It was the most modern gathering space in town, with cushioned seats and new equipment; the stage was lit by kerosene footlights. The auditorium was used for numerous events (though apparently never for opera), from temperance lectures to vaudeville shows.

January's offering, "The Scottish Reformation," was one of a series of religious-based professional stage shows written and produced by Mrs. H. D. Monroe of Washington. Though each church on her circuit recruited the actors, Mrs. Monroe provided the script, costumes, and a lecturer who between scenes would narrate slides shown on a stereoscope brought in just for the performance. (Monroe split the proceeds with the church.) A forerunner to the electric-powered slide projector, this so-called "magic lantern" produced a three-dimensional effect for scenic pictures with equipment Mrs. Monroe had used for twenty-five years. A calcium light projector was used to show the slides, with the light produced by combining two compressed gases. Mrs. Monroe usually traveled with an experienced projectionist, but this time she had to train someone new on short notice. In fact, Mrs. Monroe herself sat out the Boyertown run. Feeling under the weather, she sent her sister, Della Mayers, to serve as the lecturer for the lantern slides.

Still, the show was going well on its first night. The plot of "The Scottish Reformation" centered on the clash between the Roman Catholic Queen Mary and Scottish Puritans in the sixteenth century. As the third scene ended, the play was nearing its climax, which depicted the execution of Queen Mary and the victory of the Puritans. The actress portraying Mary had left the stage in an impressive jeweled gown, accompanied by several young girls as trainbearers. Mrs. Mayers began to describe the third series of intermission slides.

As the projectionist, Harry Fisher, fired up the magic lantern, a tube on the projector came loose, filling the auditorium with a hissing sound. This was a common problem with stereoscopes. The light was produced by combining compressed oxygen and illuminating gases, including hydrogen, which could produce hissing. Projectionists at the time had to be specially trained to control the flow of gases to avoid the noise. But Harry Fisher had received only a few days of training earlier in the month—far short of the three months most operators needed to proficiently run the machine. Fisher put his thumb over the tube to quiet the noise and fumbled to fix the hose, but the hissing continued.

The audience grew restless. Confused, several actors peeked out from behind the stage curtain and moved to the front of the stage to see what the problem was. In the process, an actor knocked over one of the kerosene footlights, starting a small fire on stage. The fire itself could have been easily contained, but it set in motion a disastrous chain of events.

Audience members grew more concerned, and some started to hurry for the exit, which was partially blocked by the projection equipment. An elderly man climbed onto his chair, pleading with the audience to remain calm, but the panic escalated, and crowds began to rush to the rear exit. As the fire reached the kerosene tank that fueled the footlights, several men, including St. John's pastor, Reverend Adam Weber, decided they should throw the tank out the window. As Reverend Weber and Mrs. Mayer pleaded with the crowd to stay calm, the men hoisted the kerosene tank toward the window. But the tank buckled, seriously burning Reverend Weber and spreading the flames. The muslin stage curtain caught fire, separating the actors from the audience by a wall of flames.

Charles Spatz, the newspaper editor and a cast member, came forward to help. As he opened the window so the tank could be thrown out, a huge flash exploded, and fire engulfed the entire auditorium. Numerous survivors reported that it seemed an explosion of fire filled the air above the audience. In a statement to the inquest that followed the disaster, Spatz said, ". . . the flames seemed to ignite suddenly a gas and the whole room was lighted in a flash. . . . I was overcome by an extreme heat and ugly smell. I groped my way to the nearest window. I got on the window ledge, opened the window and took another look back and there saw a hot, glowing flame over the whole room and everybody was dead or seemed dead. There was no woodwork burning, only the air as it seemed to me."

A number of factors made escape impossible for many. First, the auditorium was wooden from floor to ceiling, so the flames spread quickly. Second, the rear exit doors opened inward, and one of them was bolted, creating a logjam of panic as the crowds pushed to get out. Frank Cullen, a blacksmith who survived, described the scene to a Philadelphia newspaper reporter: "[There was] a terrible rush for the doors, and during the next few minutes people went crazy, knocking each other down and trampling each other underfoot. It was a battle in which the strong only had a chance to escape." Third, the stairway leading down from the second-floor theater was 6 feet wide, but it narrowed to half that at the first-floor ticket booth.

Rather than rush to leave, many in the chaos searched frantically for friends and relatives. Many cast members escaped down an exit at the rear of the stage, but that avenue was cut off for audience members by the burning curtain. A few actors, thinking the fire not that serious, returned to the auditorium to help and ended up becoming trapped themselves. Though the building did have fire escapes, they were not marked and could be accessed only by climbing 3 feet to the windowsills. A *New York Times* account the following day reported that

> . . . men and women, some carrying children in their arms, flung themselves from [the windows], risking the fall to the ground a story below. . . . To reach the windows, however, meant even a terrible fight with others, who also sought this

means of escape. Crowds surrounded every opening, pushing, striking one another, and struggling madly for the
chance to hurl themselves thirty feet to the ground. People
behind them strove to reach the windows, and many persons were pushed headlong from them without the opportunity of preparing for the jump.

Those not too seriously injured tried desperately to help
others escape. Walter Houck, a local baseball star, carried a
woman he thought was his fiancée down the fire escape, only
to discover it was another woman. He rushed back up, located
his fiancée, managed to carry her to safety, and in the end went
back to rescue several others.

A newspaper in neighboring Pottstown reported the story
of a young boy in the audience who, afraid of fire, had mapped
out in advance what he would do in just such an emergency.
When those around him began to stampede, the boy remained
calm, stepping on chairs to reach a window with a fire escape.

A Boyertown resident named William Wien testified at the
inquest that he ran up the stairway in search of his wife,
Emma. Finding the door closed, he forced it open, and a group
of panicked people fell forward. Wien estimated that he was
able to grasp twenty-five people and shove them down the
stairs.

As cries for help spread through town, fire brigades mobilized and panicked family members rushed to the scene to
determine the fate of loved ones. At the Keystone Firehouse
just several blocks away, firefighters gathered quickly and
rolled out the hose cart. Because the fire was close, the men
decided they wouldn't waste the time getting their horses from
the stable, but would pull the cart themselves. They had done

After the fire, the Rhoads Opera House was just a shell of what it had been. INSTITUTE OF AMERICAN DELTIOLOGY, MYERSTOWN, PA.

it before, and it was just a short climb up a hill and then a run downhill two blocks to the Opera House.

What they failed to consider was that the streets of Boyertown had recently been paved for the first time. As they started downhill, the cart quickly gathered speed and veered out of control. John Graver, one of the firefighters, was pinned against a tree; though his colleagues carried him to Dr. Rhoads' office, Graver died a short time later. The hose cart was too damaged to be of use at the fire scene, and by then the flames were raging out of control, and those on hand could do nothing but stand back and watch the Opera House burn.

Word of the disaster began to spread beyond Boyertown. A wire to Pottstown, 8 miles away, sent fire equipment and doctors rushing to the scene. But in the end, the fire was too ferocious, and 179 people were dead. Among them were seven cast members, and the family members of thirteen others. Harry Foreman, a member of the town council, lost five family members in the audience, though two daughters who were in the play managed to escape. William Shollenberger, a stonecutter at the Marble and Granite Works near the cemetery, was killed along with his wife and daughter-in-law; his only surviving son took over the business of carving gravestones. Some of the relief funds that poured into the town were used to buy a plot in the Fairview Cemetery to bury the unidentified dead.

Harry Fisher, the projectionist, was badly burned and later testified that he was not to blame for the fire. Mrs. Mayers, the slide narrator, was purportedly last seen helping others escape; she died in the fire.

Shortly after midnight, the roof of the Rhoads Opera House fell in with a crash, sending up sparks that ignited several nearby buildings. It would be more than four hours yet before the fires were finally brought under control.

A profound grief settled over Boyertown in the days that followed. The funerals began Thursday and continued into the following week. One local minister was reported on the verge of collapse after performing fifty-one funerals in five days. The Casket Company, one of the town's largest employers, worked overtime constructing enough caskets for its own community. A *Philadelphia Evening Bulletin* report on the aftermath focused on Stella Tabor, a schoolteacher who had the starring role in the production: "Instead of the bespangled gown, which she wore as Mary Queen of Scots, she was dressed today in black. Her eyes were swollen with weeping for her dead mother."

Editor Spatz was recovered enough by January 19 to write in his paper, "The terrible disaster caused a gloom to settle over our town which only time can dispel. The words of a certain

The gutted interior of the opera house after the fire, in which 179 people perished. INSTITUTE OF AMERICAN DELTIOLOGY, MYERSTOWN, PA.

writer, 'There is not a fireside but has some vacant chair,' are only too true."

The following year, the Pennsylvania state legislature unanimously passed two laws aimed at correcting some of the conditions that led to the disaster in Boyertown. Act 233 applied to theaters, public halls, and lodge halls with more than two stories, requiring doors that opened outward, easily accessible fire escapes, and more than one exit from second floors. In addition, the law prohibited the use of combustible materials for lighting. Act 206 required fireproof booths for projector machines and stereopticons.

A coroner's jury heard testimony from fifty witnesses, much of which was confused and contradictory to other reports. In the end, the jury found two people criminally negligent: Mrs. Monroe, the show's producer, for hiring an inexperienced projectionist, and State Factory Inspector Harry Bechtel, for failing to enforce existing fire safety laws. No charges were ever brought against the two.

The Rhoads Opera House was rebuilt and today houses apartments and retail stores.

THE SIGHT WAS INDESCRIBABLE

Eddystone and Oakdale Explosions
1917, 1918

Eddystone, April 10, 1917

On April 6, 1917, the United States declared war against Germany and formally entered the escalating conflict in Europe. Just four days later, on April 10, a devastating series of explosions ripped through an ammunitions plant on the outskirts of Philadelphia that had ramped up production to supply the troops with bullets. Was it an act of wartime sabotage or simply a horrible accident?

The Eddystone Ammunition Corporation employed thousands of workers and had recently doubled its workforce to increase production for the war effort. Many of Eddystone's employees were girls and young women whose job it was to load shells with explosive black powder. The loading plant where the explosion occurred was known as "F" Building and consisted of three main areas: a "pellet room" where workers made black powder fuses that ran through shrapnel shells, a loading room where the shells were loaded with explosive powder, and a final room where inspectors checked the quality of the finished product. At about 10 A.M. on Monday, April 10, something went terribly wrong in F Building.

William Drayer, a worker at the plant, had just asked a fellow worker the time. "I had no sooner turned back to my desk than the first explosion occurred," he told a reporter for the *New York Times*. "The first one sounded like the explosion of a five-gallon can of gasoline." That first explosion was quickly followed by two more, as flames spread throughout the explosive-filled room. "When the third explosion occurred I was blown through the door near my desk," Drayer continued. "After regaining consciousness, I noticed the flames bursting out of the structure. I saw a girl rush out with her clothing in flames. She stumbled and fell, and I tried to pick her up, but I was so weak that I also fell."

The sounds of chaos filled the air, as did the sound of continuing smaller explosions. Some workers, like Drayer, had been blown through doors and windows to safety. Others ran for their lives. David Heesner, chief of the Eddystone Fire Company, related his experience to a reporter for the *Philadelphia Inquirer*: "Bodies, shells, wood, and debris filled the air at the same moment. . . . We could see bodies that had been tossed fifty yards to the flats. Shells came whizzing through the air, bullets whistled like skyrockets and we kept ducking them. . . . The victims were horrible to behold. They were burned on face and body and in many cases were with little clothing."

Bodies were found hundreds of yards from the scene of the blast. Almost all the survivors related gruesome details about coworkers who lost their lives; many reported severed limbs and charred skin. Fifty-five of those killed that day were so badly injured that they could never be identified. In all, 133 people were killed in the explosions, mostly girls and young women. A Philadelphia reporter witnessed a young girl who escaped the initial blast but was then struck by an exploding shell. "It made a deep gash in her head and penetrated the skull. As she was lifted down by one of the Eddystone plant guards she died in his arms."

David Crocket escaped without serious injuries. He told the *New York Times,* "There was no warning of what was coming. I was thrown to the floor at the first flash, and the bodies of half a dozen other men fell on top of me. Most of them were dead, I think. These bodies saved my life."

Workers employed in other parts of the plant rushed to F Building and tried to help victims out of the burning building. The call for help went out for firefighters, ambulances, and doctors throughout the city to rush to the scene. Anthony Zatek, an assistant foreman at the plant, had the day off but happened to be driving by when the first explosion occurred. "Almost immediately I heard the screams of the girls," he told a Philadelphia reporter. "They were heart-rending. Realizing that something serious had happened I sped my car to the plant. . . . The sight that greeted me was awful—indescribable." Zatek rushed to work, loading victims of the blast into his car. In all, he made seven trips to a nearby hospital before he himself was injured by an exploding shell.

Captain W. M. Wilhelm, the general manager of the plant, rushed from his office and assisted victims to safety. He later praised the acts of many plant workers who helped in the rescue effort; some stood on top of a powder magazine wetting it down with a hose to prevent it from exploding. "All the men acted as heroes. There is no doubt that prompt actions of the guards prevented a much greater loss of life and saved the fire from spreading to other buildings," Wilhelm said that day.

"Especially this is true of the manner in which men risked their lives to prevent flames from reaching the smokeless powder magazine, less than two hundred yards away from the destroyed building."

The fire at the plant burned through the afternoon, while the injured were taken to several hospitals nearby. When those hospitals became too crowded, victims were treated at a nearby National Guard Armory. James Friel, an inspector at the plant who was not injured, used a milk truck to make four trips carrying bodies to the morgue. It would be 9 P.M. before family and friends would be admitted to the morgue to identify their loved ones.

It was Captain Wilhelm, the plant's manager, who first raised the question of what caused the chain of explosions, saying he was convinced it was not the carelessness of his employees. His feelings were echoed by S. M. Vauclain, Eddystone's president, who hurried to Philadelphia from New York. "I am absolutely convinced that the explosion was not due to any accidental cause," Mr. Vauclain told reporters late in the day. "We have received many reports that some outside person was responsible for the disaster, and we are examining all of these."

In the days that followed, many pointed fingers at the Germans and the Russians, claiming sabotage. There were reports that a telegram was sent from Eddystone to a radical Russian newspaper in New York immediately after the explosions. One plant official told the *New York Times* the explosions "were the result of a diabolical plot conceived in the degenerate brain of a demon in human guise." A Trenton, New Jersey, woman told police she found a note in Philadelphia's Broad Street Station discussing a plot to blow up the munitions works. But a coroner's jury convened to investigate the blast found that there was not enough credible evidence to support the theory of a plot, and the cause of the disaster remains a mystery.

The Eddystone Ammunition Corporation paid for the fifty-five unidentified victims of the explosions to be buried in a mass grave site in the Chester Rural Cemetery. A funeral service was held there on April 13, and an estimated 12,000 people gathered in the cemetery to pay their respects. In less than two weeks, the plant was back in operation, making ammunition for the war effort.

Oakdale, May 18, 1918

Just one year later, outside of Pittsburgh, another factory supplying the U.S. armed forces with explosives was also the scene of a disastrous blast. A report the following day in the *Philadelphia Inquirer* called the event "one of the greatest and most kaleidoscopic explosion catastrophes in the history of the Pittsburgh district."

The Aetna Chemical Company plant in Oakdale manufactured the explosives TNT and TNA. At about noon on May 18, 1918, as some of the plant's workmen were settling into their lunch hour, they heard "a report not much louder than the crack of a pistol." Still, knowing the danger, the workers suspected trouble and hurried for the doors. H. H. Canan was just sitting down to lunch when the first explosion hit. "I was sitting with two friends about 100 feet from the TNT stock room when the blast came," he told a newspaper reporter. "I lost consciousness. When I hit the ground I came to. My two friends landed about 100 feet from me. I got to my feet and was hurrying away when I came to an injured man. I put him on my back and started from the plant, when the second explosion occurred."

That second explosion devastated the factory. As reported in *The New York Times*, "Before they could gain the open the very air seemed to burst into flames, the earth heaved and rocked, and, with a roar that was heard for miles, the long factory buildings were hurled high into the air, carrying with them ponderous equipment and scores of men." The bodies of some of those killed in the blast were found as far as a half-mile from the buildings where they had been working.

The factory immediately burst into flames, and additional explosions rocked the wreckage as the heat spread to tanks holding TNT and TNA. A cloud of smoke and toxic fumes rose over the site, blanketing the small valley and surrounding community. Residents of a nearby borough would later describe the scene as "resembling the eruption of a volcano." The explosion had brought down telephone and telegraph wires, so an Aetna employee had to hurry to nearby Carnegie to alert firefighters and rescue workers. The call went out for help, and hospitals in the area and in Pittsburgh sent doctors and nurses to the scene. For a time, the intense heat, fumes, and fear of further explosions held rescuers at bay.

Surgeon J. A. Hanna arrived on the first relief train, and was met by a "living hell." He told a *New York Times* reporter flames were shooting hundreds of feet into the air and that bodies of victims could be seen as far as a mile away. As he pulled out on a train now loaded with victims, Dr. Hanna said the train had to race through the flames, which were inching closer to an unexploded tank of TNT.

By now anxious family members were hurrying to the scene for news of their loved ones, and police also reported that the huge explosion drew curious onlookers from miles around. The State Constabulary rushed officers in from Greensburg to help cordon off the burning factory, letting in only those who could help. Sheriff William Haddock was one of the first on the scene; he was thrown to the ground by an explosion and just missed being hit by a flying piece of steel.

Among the first medical personnel to arrive was a crew from St. John's Hospital in Pittsburgh, the closest to Oakdale. Dr. L. W. Milford brought along Marlyne Ashelman, a twenty-one-year-old nurse. According to a report in the *Philadelphia Inquirer,* police tried to hold them back, but they insisted on approaching several injured workmen lying not far from an unexploded tank. The tank exploded just as Dr. Milford and Ashelman reached the injured men, and Dr. Milford was thrown 50 feet into a ditch. He found Ashelman lying 40 feet away, only partly conscious. Her right leg had been blown off. She was later hailed as one of the great heroes of the rescue effort at Oakdale.

Most of the injured were rushed to hospitals in Pittsburgh. It so happened that the city was hosting a Red Cross parade that day for nurses about to be dispatched to France to help in the war effort. Once they learned what had happened, nurses from the parade went immediately to help as victims were carried from the trains to emergency vehicles. *The Philadelphia Inquirer* reported that dozens of Red Cross nurses, dressed in their white uniforms, had been traveling to the parade when they heard the explosion and detoured instead to the factory to help.

The fire continued to burn throughout the day, and the last of a reported nine explosions occurred at about 6:30 P.M., scattering the wreckage and destruction even further. According to one reporter, that final explosion "swept away the remnants of the fire and practically cleared the blackened space." A group of mine rescuers arrived from the arsenal station of the U.S. Bureau of Mines with special equipment and oxygen masks to help hunt for survivors. Then came the grim task of trying to identify the victims. The coroner, Samuel C. Jamison, determined that the most effective way to figure out who had died in the blast was to conduct a census of the town of Oakdale. Survivors were asked to register at a special office, where residents could also report missing family members. Thousands arrived at a temporary morgue in search of information. A report in the May 20 edition of the *New York Times* related the sad story of Adam Partz, who was working with the coroner. According to the reporter, Partz collapsed when "he found in a bucket a bunch of keys and a penknife which had belonged to his son. The son had been employed at the plant."

The final death toll from the explosion and fire was 193 people, which included several rescuers who were overcome by the fumes or struck by objects during an explosion. Hundreds more were seriously injured. Many of the victims were buried in the Oakdale Cemetery, where a large monument was placed. It reads: "Erected by the Aetna Chemical Company, in memory of those employees who lost their lives in the explosion at the Oakdale plant, May 18, 1918. Their lives were devoted to the manufacture of materials necessary to the United States in the Prosecution of the war against Germany. Like soldiers they died in their country's service."

AN ACCIDENT LEADS TO TRAGEDY

The Chester Bridge Collapse

1921

No one was sure what first drew the three-year-old boy to the edge of the Chester River that day, September 10, 1921. Someone said he was watching a group of boys swimming; another thought that perhaps he had climbed into a leaky rowboat tied up on the shore and that the boat had sunk under his weight. Whatever happened, at about 7:00 that night, Gus Apostolos ended up in the water, and the calls for help set in motion a tragic chain of events.

A man named Thomas Hemsworth later told police what had happened. "I was about to go into the Edgmont Theater," Hemsworth recalled, "when a small boy came running toward me, telling me between sobs, that a boy had fallen into the river in the back of the Story Coal Company." He ran to the river, where he was joined by John Perry, a former fire truck driver. They grabbed whatever they could to try to rescue the boy, hoisting long poles and trying to get the boy to grab hold.

As more people called for help, a crowd began to form. Police arrived with grappling hooks and rowboats, and some

*The Third Street Bridge looks idyllic in this undated postcard
from before the chain-reaction tragedy began.*

dove into the river to search for the boy. Panicked mothers ran
to the scene and before long, more than sixty people had
crowded onto the Third Street Bridge to watch the frantic rescue attempts in the river below. A report the next day in the
Philadelphia Inquirer said that "the jam on the footpath became
so thick that passage was impossible as spectators watched the
divers at work." Some said the bridge was vibrating slightly,
but that was mostly ignored as the drama unfolded.

Suddenly, a large section of the wooden footpath on the
thirty-year-old bridge collapsed, sending the crowds hurtling 15
feet into the water. Among those who fell into the river were a
number of mothers who had been holding small children. An
account in the following day's *New York Times* read, "In an
instant those who had gathered on the bridge were a mass of
tangled humanity, fighting for life in the murky waters of the

river. Expert swimmers were among them, but they were unable to make a single stroke for themselves or for others. Those who went over first were without even the slightest hope of rescue. They were crushed to the very bottom of the river and there were imbedded in the mud."

An eleven-year-old boy named Jacob Sapovits was riding his bicycle near the river when the bridge collapsed. Years later, Sapovits, then a lawyer, recalled the horrors of the day. "I hastened to the scene and saw people struggling in the water," he said. "It's a scene I'll never forget."

People clung to the bridge's stone supports and the parts of the bridge still standing, while onlookers dove into the water. A Chester resident named Emanuel Vadvarka was a strong swimmer; he grabbed a struggling woman by the hair and swam her to shore, then returned two more times, rescuing three small boys. Another hero that day was George Pierce, who would later become a policeman in Chester; he was credited with saving fifteen lives. Members of a theatrical company who were to perform that night at the nearby Edgmont Theater also rushed into the water. One actor dragged twenty-three people from the water; nine of them were dead. A slight man named James Silverstein held on to one of the bridge's iron railings with one hand, holding tight to a woman with the other, until bystanders could lead her to safety.

Those who owned automobiles and trucks rushed to the scene to help carry the injured to Chester Hospital. Three men who worked in a garage just feet from the bridge were alerted by the screams and backed a truck up to the shore within minutes. Some of the bodies pulled from the water were limp and lifeless. Others struggled to breathe. A neighborhood doctor, Joseph DiMedio, stayed by the shore providing mouth-to-mouth resuscitation to victims as they emerged from the water. Dr. DiMedio had been practicing medicine for only a year from his office on West Third Street in Chester. He worked more than seven hours that night trying to revive victims, with the help of the Chester City Comptroller, Albert Hughes.

As darkness began to fall, police brought in searchlights from nearby shipyards to flood the area with light, and many people with automobiles trained their headlights on the river. Divers were sent to the river bottom to recover bodies. Realizing that the tide was rising, firemen used 40-foot ladders to construct a barrier in the water. They covered it with fishing nets to prevent any bodies from being washed away toward the bay with the rising tide.

In the end, more than fifty people, many of them children, were pulled out alive, but twenty-four men, women, and children lost their lives in the waters of the Chester River. Police had difficulty containing the crowds that descended on the scene and at Chester Hospital, where most of the survivors were taken. People were frantic for word about family and friends. A reporter for the *Philadelphia Inquirer* recorded the scene at the hospital, where a crowd had gathered to await word:

> Suddenly the clanging of a bell would break the silence, and a motor patrol wagon with its deathly freight would dash madly up to the entrance. With a huge sigh that seemed to spread throughout the entire assembly, the crowd would surge forward, peering anxiously at each somber form lifted from the wagon and carried up the steps to the yawning doors waiting to receive it. As one or another in the throng would recognize a familiar face or perhaps a well-known

article of clothing, a muffled sob would break forth, only to be choked back as the police, mercifully ruthless, pressed back the too-eager individual. Then, as the last stretcher was taken from the wagon and the wooden doors crashed shut in their anguished faces, the crowds settled back once more into the old attitudes of patient suffering, waiting for the news that the next load of bodies might bring.

One man who made his way into the hospital was Leroy Hawkins, a railroad worker. He arrived just as doctors were reviving his wife. As she regained consciousness, Hawkins went to examine a row of bodies that had been placed nearby, covered with white sheets. "The man drew back the sheet and found himself looking at the faces of his two children," the *Philadelphia Inquirer* reporter wrote. "With a shriek, he fainted. When he was revived the first thing he said was to beg physicians and nurses not to tell his wife that the children had been drowned."

Among those drowned were forty-five-year-old Maude Murtha, who was walking to her son's house with a present for her granddaughter, and Morris Knopf, the owner of a nearby pawnshop, who just the day before had decided to postpone a trip planned for that day to New Jersey. The last body recovered from the river was that of Gus Apostolos—the three-year-old boy whose fatal foray into the river precipitated the entire tragedy.

Ultimately, it was determined that the accident's cause could be traced to a day twelve years earlier when a coal barge rammed the bridge's foundation, bending and cracking a plate that supported one of the bridge's steel beams. At the time, workers removed the plate and tried to straighten it, instead splitting it even more in the process. Despite the crack, the plate was bolted back into place. After the accident, there were reports that the bridge had been inspected just ten months earlier. The wooden footpath had been patched in several places, but no one made any repairs to the cracked plate.

CHAPTER 10

"HYSTERIA WAS EVERYWHERE"

The Crash of the Congressional Limited

1943

In the early 1940s, with the country at war, much of the nation's attention and financial resources were focused overseas. In addition, many men of working age were serving in the armed forces, depleting the workforce at home. The country's infrastructure was starting to suffer, as reduced maintenance and staff shortages took their toll. In the first six months of 1943, the number of railway accidents rose more than 30 percent, to 8,209.

Releasing those frightening statistics in a report, the Interstate Commerce Commission said that at least half of the incidents could be traced to improper maintenance, and stressed that those numbers would decline if "the urge to keep trains moving were not permitted to take precedence over safety." Just the week before Labor Day, a Delaware, Lackawanna and Western passenger train had derailed in Wayland, New York, killing twenty-seven people and injuring seventy-five.

Traffic on the railroads was particularly heavy over Labor Day weekend in 1943, as families traveled to be together and many servicemen were given the holiday off. The situation was no different on the Pennsylvania Railroad's premier line, the Congressional Limited, which ran the important route between Washington, D.C., and New York City. Expecting a crush of riders on each of the Limited's Labor Day runs on September 6, the railroad added up to sixteen extra cars per train to handle the crowds. When the 4 P.M. train pulled out of Washington, there were 541 people onboard, many of them soldiers home on leave.

The train made good time and was running ahead of schedule by the time it reached Philadelphia. The conductor slowed to 45 miles per hour through the congested city and past the North Philadelphia Station on North Broad Street. Trouble was just ahead.

Shortly after 6 P.M., a worker in a rail yard 3 miles east of the North Philadelphia Station in the Kensington section of the city looked up as the Congressional Limited passed by. Harold McClintoc noticed something wrong. Smoke and flames were shooting from a journal box on one of the cars. Journal boxes held the train's metal axles, using oil to reduce the heat and friction, but this one was overheating. McClintoc hollered to a coworker, A. J. Carlin, to alert the next signal tower to the problem so they could stop the train. Carlin hurried to the telephone to call the signal man, but the phone rang just as the train roared past.

A few seconds later, the burning journal box on the train's seventh car locked up, snapping the front axle in two and catapulting the car vertically into the upright of a signal tower. Before crashing back onto the tracks, the car's roof was ripped off along the line of windows by the steel frame of the signal bridge. A report in the following day's *Philadelphia Inquirer* said, "The seventh car, a coach, left the rails, shot directly up into the air, tearing down every electric wire along the right-of-way, and came down like a split melon, its forward part crashing into the signal tower alongside, knocking the tower partly from its base."

The next car on the train plowed into the wrecked car with such force that it wrapped around the tower in a U-shape. The next six cars flew off the tracks as high-voltage wires on the signal bridge snapped, showering the scene below with sparks and hot wires. "The train came to a sudden stop after there had been some jerking," Navy seaman George Davis told a *New York Times* reporter on the scene. "There was a lot of screaming. I managed to climb out of the window and I noticed that my car had cracked up against a trestle. . . . I climbed through the window back into the car and helped [several passengers] out. Then I went in and saw a Negro soldier, apparently dead. He was badly mangled. I couldn't stand it any more and I had to quit."

There were more than fifty passengers riding in the seventh car; they hadn't stood a chance. Bodies and debris from the wreckage were strewn over a four-block area, with many people trapped inside train cars and screaming for help. "The car seemed to twist two or three ways at once," said Barbara Peterson. "I was thrown from my seat and my baggage and a lot of broken glass fell all around me. The car was twisted sidewise and tilted so far over that I could step right on the ground. Another car was almost on top of it." She had been seated ahead of a sailor and his family. The sailor also climbed out of a window, handed his baby to Peterson, then went back to rescue his wife.

Joseph Haiken was headed home to Brooklyn that day. "I jumped down and ran along the tracks to the diner to find my wife. The diner was still on the tracks, but was all smashed up inside," Haiken told a New York reporter. "I found my wife. She was hysterical and screamed that two or three babies in the diner had been killed. The car in front of the diner was sideways across the track and by this time they were pulling out bodies of the dead."

Police, fire crews, and teams of doctors and nurses from the closest hospitals descended on the area, and forty priests from the nearby St. Joan of Arc and St. Joachim's Catholic Churches rushed to administer last rites to the victims. Those on the train who were not badly hurt, many of them servicemen, ran to help, and nearby residents who had heard sounds of the crash quickly joined in the rescue. The *Philadelphia Inquirer* asked Kos Semonski to write about his experience. "I was about a block and a half away from Frankford Junction when I head a thunderous crash, followed by a grinding of steel," Semonski wrote. "I dropped what I was doing and rushed to the tracks. . . . Walking up and down the tracks, blood streaming down their faces, were children crying for their mothers. . . . Hysteria was everywhere. Nobody, it seemed, could think. Most of the victims lay helpless, some outside the cars, but many more inside—trapped tight by twisting metal."

The first rescuers to arrive had difficulty reaching the derailed cars because of the downed power lines. When they could, those on the train struggled to free other passengers who were pinned in their seats. Along with the police came workers from the nearby Cramps Shipyard, bringing with them acetylene torches. They went to work cutting through the mangled rail cars and were still on the job after midnight.

"Most of the women in the car became hysterical, but the servicemen climbed around among the seats and quieted them," recalled Carolyn Brown, who had been traveling to New York for a date with a marine ensign. "I was lying there on the side of the car. Finally some of the sailors pulled me out." An Army major who had been on the train organized the rescue efforts of the servicemen, while police set up spotlights and a loudspeaker to direct rescue crews. Ambulances lined the roads surrounding the tracks, and police even commandeered motorists along Castor and Kensington Avenues to take the injured to the hospital. In two cases, doctors had to amputate the legs of trapped passengers to free them from the wreckage. The bodies of the dead were lined up along the side to be taken to a temporary morgue set up in the basement of Frankford Hospital. Hospitals treating the wounded issued an urgent appeal for blood but then reported that so many donors responded to the appeals that they had to be turned away at Frankford Hospital.

Twenty-five-year-old Christina Nix was traveling home to Long Island City on the Congressional Limited. She was pinned during the crash in a standing position. It took five hours of work to free her, with doctors on the scene giving her a blood transfusion and frequent doses of morphine. According to a report in the *Philadelphia Inquirer*, Nix was conscious throughout the entire time. Once, with the heat and fumes from workers' acetylene torches becoming unbearable, a fireman told her he was going to spray her with water, at which point, Nix said, "I'm Irish. I can take it." So desperate were newspapers for some good news amid all this tragedy that they prominently featured the story of Nix's rescue in the following morning's papers. Unfortunately she died that same morning at Episcopal Hospital, just ten hours after her rescue. Philadelphia's chief police surgeon said, "She was the bravest girl I ever saw. She wouldn't give up."

Rescuers worked through the night, and it took a full twenty-four hours to remove all the dead from the wreckage. In the end, seventy-eight passengers and one dining-room employee lost their lives in the crash, all of whom were riding in the train's seventh and eighth cars. More than one hundred suffered serious injuries. Many of those who survived the disaster praised the servicemen onboard the train for holding down the hysteria and getting the early rescue efforts underway. "Cut and bleeding themselves, these men of our Nation's armed forces pitched in and worked, brushing aside offers of first aid from doctors and nurses who arrived on the scene within a few minutes," wrote Kos Semonski in the *Inquirer*. "They climbed in through car windows, freed passengers pinned under crushed seats and handed them out the windows to police. . . . Time and again I saw them refuse assistance when it seemed as if they had lost so much blood they must 'fold up.'" Philadelphia Mayor Bernard Samuel added his official praise of the servicemen, as well as the shipyard workers who rushed to the scene with their acetylene torches.

There is one other death that can be blamed on the crash of the Congressional Limited, though it wasn't listed in the official tally. Morris Borden was in his Brooklyn home when he learned that his wife and two children had been involved in a crash in Philadelphia. He traveled to the morgue, where he identified their bodies, then went home, closed his kitchen windows, and turned on his gas oven.

"MURDERED BY WHAT WAS IN THE AIR"

The Donora Smog Crisis
1948

It didn't occur to anyone to cancel Saturday's football game. In the small town of Donora, they were used to the heavy fogs that frequently blanketed the valley. And this was a big game—homecoming—with the hometown Donora Dragons facing their archrivals from Monongahela High. But as the teams lined up for the kick-off on Saturday, October 30, 1948, the crowds in the stands couldn't see the field. No passes were thrown that day because receivers couldn't see the ball. Punts disappeared into a dense fog that had hung over Donora for the past four days.

Still, the game went on, judging by the whistles of the referees. At some point, the game announcer called for the Dragons' star tight end, Stanley Sawa, to hurry home, and he ran down the hill toward his house, still in his uniform. Sawa's father had been brought home from the mill short of breath, and by the time his son reached home he was dead. The people of Donora were starting to realize that something was terribly wrong in their town.

A blue-collar town on the Monongahela River about 25 miles south of Pittsburgh, Donora was nestled between ridges of the Allegheny Mountains. What with the river and the industrial plants in town, people were accustomed to heavy fog and pollution. Bill Schempp, a Donora fireman, said the horns of steamboats were a constant sound for residents, and this fog on the river caused many boat collisions. But about the pollution, Schempp said, "We lived in it. We accepted it."

The town didn't have much choice. In the 1940s, Donora had a population of about 14,000, the majority of them immigrants employed by the American Steel & Wire plant and the U.S. Steel Corporation's Zinc Works, which dominated the area. The factories provided jobs and kept families fed. The 4-mile-long Zinc smelting plant by the river employed 6,500 people at its peak, and smog and smelly air were just the price people had to pay for jobs in the valley. A sign at the factory gate boasted, "The World's Largest Nail Mill." Beyond grousing about dirty curtains, trouble growing gardens, and having to repaint houses often because of the corrosive smoke, no one thought too much about it.

The problems in Donora that October rolled into the valley slowly—literally with the fog—on Tuesday the 26th. What happened is now technically called a temperature inversion—descending cold air that prevents warm air from rising. In Donora, that inversion was acting like a heavy, wet blanket, trapping the noxious fumes spewing from the smokestacks at the Zinc Works. (A similar inversion was blamed for 4,000 deaths in London in 1952.)

Over the next several days, the air got thicker and thicker. Automobiles crept through the town with their headlights on, and streetlights shone at midday, trying to cut through the fog.

Wire mills spewing smoke along the Monongahela River on an ordinary day in Donora. LIBRARY OF CONGRESS, LC-USZ62-131258

Arnold Hirsh, an attorney on Main Street, remembers "The air looked yellow, never like that before. Nothing moved. . . . I went over . . . looking down toward the river, and you could just barely see the railroad tracks. Right there on the tracks was a coal-burning engine puffing away. It issued a big blast of black smoke that went up about 6 feet in the air and stopped cold. It just hung there, with no place to go, in air that did not move."

Though some people in town weren't feeling well, life in Donora went on. The annual Halloween parade was held as scheduled on Friday, with costumed children disappearing into an appropriately spooky haze. The mother of Devra Davis, a Donora native who wrote 2002's *When Smoke Ran Like Water*, said, "The fog was heavy, but there was only one Halloween every year. Only this time, we could not see much." The football team practiced that afternoon for its big game the next day,

but the coach had to yell "Kick!" so receivers would know there
was a ball on the way. Though reports on the radio were starting to warn about the "smog"—a term unfamiliar to most at
the time—no one paid much attention. Henry Loftus was driving home to Donora that night and said he had to stick his
head out of his car window to try to see through the fog. He
gave up and stayed with a friend.

By the end of the homecoming game on Saturday, nine people in Donora had died. That number would double within
twenty-four hours. The town's eight doctors were getting panicked calls, but there was little they could do. Arnold Hirsh
called Dr. William Rongaus because his ailing mother couldn't
catch her breath. "He said that he just could not make it," Hirsh
recalled. "He said, 'The whole town is sick. Even healthy fellas
are dropping. Get your mother the hell out of town!'" Dr. Rongaus was giving the same advice to the many concerned patients
who were calling, but there was one problem: The roads were
packed, and the fog was so heavy that drivers could hardly see.
Still, some people were unaware of the danger. John Lignelli was
sitting on a bench outside the borough building when a delivery
truck from Pittsburgh rolled through. The truck crews were
wearing emergency breathing devices. "We asked them why
they were wearing respirators," Lignelli said. "They said because
the air is bad. I said, 'We don't have a problem here.'"

But others were increasingly alarmed. The town burgess
declared a state of emergency, and doctors urged all those who
couldn't leave to stay inside with the windows and doors closed
tight. Bill Schempp remembers driving down the ridge road on
Saturday evening, surrounded by fog. "It was like going into a
sink hole," he said. He remembers seeing lights on in the basement of the community center and thinking it was odd that

someone was there that late at night. He didn't know that the community center had been turned into a temporary morgue.

Later that night, fire bells rang out, calling emergency crews in to help. The Donora Fire Department and volunteer firefighters from nearby communities kicked into action. They tied handkerchiefs over their noses and mouths and went from house to house toting heavy oxygen tanks. Schempp was one of those firemen. "You can't imagine what it was like. You couldn't see your hand in front of your face," he remembers. "It took us at least one hour to go to someone's home only five blocks away. We had to feel our way along the fence." Still, there was not enough oxygen to go around, so firefighters had to limit how much they gave at each stop. Schempp recalls that as soon as they'd take the oxygen away, victims would start to wheeze again, gasping for air. They'd give them a few more breaths of oxygen, then move on to the next call. Schempp recalls someone saying, "I'm dying and you're taking my air from me."

Fireman John Volk arranged to borrow additional oxygen canisters from the fire departments in nearby Monongahela, Monessen, and Charleroi. "There never was such fog," Volk said. "Hell, even inside the station the air was blue. I drove on the left side of the street with my head out the window, steering by scraping the curb."

The Monongahela Memorial and Charleroi–Monessen Hospitals were besieged by people complaining of trouble breathing. Many also had severe abdominal cramps, horrible headaches, and vomiting. Some who already suffered from respiratory problems began coughing up blood. And it wasn't just the people in the valley who were suffering. Family pets were falling over. Houseplants were dying. Cows and chickens in

The mills continued operating for a full week after the deadly smog settled over the town of Donora. NATIONAL LIBRARY OF MEDICINE

the nearby farms of Webster fell dead in the fields.

Doctor Rongaus noticed that some of the people who could make it up to Palmer Park, which sat high on a hill, seemed to get better, and he recruited some in town to transport victims there. "My brother and I hauled women . . . in horse-drawn wagons up to the park," he said. "Soon as we got them above the smog, they would get much better." Nearby residents provided food and blankets to those camping out in the park.

Broadcaster Walter Winchell began his national radio broadcast that Saturday night in his booming voice: "Good evening, America! The small, hard-working steel town of Donora, Pennsylvania, is in mourning tonight, as they recover from a catastrophe. People dropped dead from a thick killer fog that sickened much of the town." Once word of the disaster got out, phone lines into Donora were jammed, with some residents having to wait hours to talk to relatives.

Still, the mills were running day and night. It was not until Sunday morning—Halloween day—that U.S. Steel finally shut down the Zinc Works. By then, the town's funeral home had run out of caskets. Twenty people were dead and 6,000 people—more than one-third of Donora's population—were sick or hospitalized. Within a month, seventy people had died.

Finally, early on the morning of November 1, the skies opened. It rained hard all day, and the fog cleared. Funerals for most of the victims were held the following day, under clear blue skies. Doctor Rongaus would later say that if the smog had lasted just another twenty-four hours, the death toll could have been in the thousands. "These people were murdered by whatever was in the air. There's nothing else you can call it," he said. "There's something in the air here that isn't found anywhere else."

It didn't take long for investigators to descend on Donora to find out what had gone wrong. They pointed the finger of blame at the Zinc Works, saying the smog had been a poisonous mix of sulfur dioxide, carbon monoxide, and heavy metal dusts pouring from the smokestacks. U.S. Steel denied any responsibility, blaming instead "an act of God." To this day, its records remain sealed. (The company settled hundreds of claims out of court.) But as a reporter for the *Monessen Daily Independent* wrote at the time, "You didn't need science to identify the culprit. All you needed was a pair of reasonably good eyes."

Still, the following week, the Zinc Works was back in business. However, the investigations that followed marked the first time the government got involved in an organized effort to determine the health impacts of air pollution. The tragedy that hit Donora would later be called "the Hiroshima of air pollution." In 1998, on the fiftieth anniversary of the incident, John Lignelli, now mayor of Donora, stated, "It was on account of what happened here that opened the eyes of the federal government that they needed to do something. Donora should take credit for that."

In 1949 President Harry Truman called for a national conference on air pollution, and, in 1955 Congress passed the country's first Clean Air Act. It is estimated that during the Donora smog incident, emissions of sulfur dioxide ranged up to 5,500 micrograms per cubic meter. Current regulations mandate no more than 80 micrograms per cubic meter.

Though the Zinc Works did not shut down for good until 1957, that week in October 1948 spelled the beginning of the end for Donora. A long-running series of factory closings devastated the local economy, and the current population of the town has dropped to 5,000. Many of the people who had lived there at the time reported a lifetime of health problems. A report in the *New York Times* in 1966 said, "Time has added an ominous footnote. A survey of the town ten years after the inversion showed that the mortality and illness rates for those affected by the smog had consistently remained higher than for the unaffected portion of the population."

At a hillside church service held on the fiftieth anniversary of the tragedy, environmental officials joined local townspeople to honor the victims of the Donora smog. A local high school student successfully campaigned to have the state erect a historical marker near the former mill. At the time, environmental historian Ken Wolensky of the Pennsylvania Historical and Museum Commission in Harrisburg said, "The Donora smog played a significant role in sparking the environmental movement. It marked the beginning of government stepping in to examine just what industrial pollution might be doing to people."

A FUN OUTING GOES HORRIBLY WRONG

The Wreck of the Phillies Special

1962

It started out as a wonderful excursion. A bunch of baseball fans from the Harrisburg area were climbing onboard a train, heading to the big city to see the Philadelphia Phillies take on the Pittsburgh Pirates. Two Pennsylvania baseball teams playing in front of a Pennsylvania crowd. Destination: Connie Mack Stadium in North Philadelphia.

The Pennsylvania Railroad's Phillies Special pulled out of Harrisburg shortly after 5 P.M. on July 28, 1962, with 140 people onboard. The passengers included a Little League team traveling to the game together and many other children. Cloyd Mark and his wife, Florence, had driven 50 miles to Harrisburg from Mifflinburg. Their nine-year-old grandson was visiting from Lubbock, Texas, and had never seen a major league ball game. The boy's father called it a once-in-a-lifetime vacation. They were to make stops at Elizabethville, Coatesville, and Lancaster along the way to pick up more fans before arriving in Philadelphia for an evening game.

David Wilbert was a smelter foreman at the Bethlehem Steel Company in Steelton, just outside of Harrisburg. He was standing at the end of a crane watching a crew working on the nearby railroad tracks when he saw the Phillies Special come into view. "I saw the engine and five cars go by, but the sixth caught a pole," he told a reporter for the *Philadelphia Inquirer*. "It kept on going and then hit a second and third pole before it fishtailed and went down the embankment." Powered by two diesel engines, the train had gotten up to 70 miles per hour as it neared the steel plant. When the rear cars whiplashed off the tracks, three of the nine cars tumbled down a 40-foot embankment into the waters of the Susquehanna River. Wilbert ran to call the police. He later said his fifteen-year-old son Jerome had wanted to go on the baseball outing, but Wilbert had vetoed the idea because it would get him home too late.

W. K. Besteder, the brakeman on the train, told reporters, "It was a happy crowd. It was a crowd going to a ball game. I felt in high spirits myself because I planned to see the game, too. The train crew usually gets to see a few innings, anyhow." But then the cars went flying, and screams filled the train.

Cloyd Mark had his arm around his grandson, whose clothes were covered in mud, when he spoke to reporters at a hospital in Harrisburg. "I was going to treat the family to a ball game. I never saw a big league game before in my life. This was to be the first one." The family had just settled into the second-to-last car on the train and was waiting to give the conductor their tickets. "All of a sudden we felt a bump," Mark said. "The car rolled on the right side and filled up with water. Mrs. Mark, my wife, was pinned under a seat about at her chest. I tried to pull the seat off and my son tried to pull her free but we couldn't get her loose."

He continued, "Finally, the police broke out the rest of the window where we were sitting and some other men pulled me out. They told me my wife was dead and there was nothing else I could do for her."

Mark's grandson, Lyman, also spoke with reporters. "My daddy and me and my grandmom and grandpop were going to see the baseball game," he said. "My daddy's shoulder was hurt, but they wouldn't tell me how bad. I don't know how it happened. All I know is grandmom is dead."

The cars in the river came to rest along the shoreline in about 2 feet of water. The death toll in the accident would likely have been much higher had the area not been in the middle of a drought. Police at the scene said that had the Susquehanna been at its regular level—about 6 feet near the shore—more passengers would have drowned in the overturned coaches. But the drought conditions did present another problem; brush on the side of the track caught fire when high-voltage lines came crashing down, and several small fires had to be extinguished.

Nineteen-year-old John Wilcox of Selinsgrove was traveling with a friend, Robert Burd, to see his first Phillies game. "I was just riding along and then I felt a bump," Wilcox said. "The train went over a bank and the next thing I knew the car was full of water. We were lucky being in the last car. We got out the rear door and just waded to shore."

Though both boys were slightly hurt, they walked away from the accident. "The first thing I knew the seats started to fly," Burd told a Philadelphia reporter. Once they reached shore, the boys were told to lie on the ground and wait for help. He said that by that time, "rescuers flew fast and thick" among the victims.

Police and ambulance crews were on the scene quickly, helped in their rescue efforts by several boaters who had been on the river when the crash occurred. Dr. H. R. Ward was onboard the first ambulance that reached the site. "The scene hit me like a bomb as I leaped from the ambulance and ran toward the overturned cars of the train," Dr. Ward told a reporter. "When we got inside the coaches, we found others under water in there. I would say at least 10 were dead, but I didn't have time to count." Ward described the passengers sitting on the riverbank as "in positions that gave one the impression of idleness . . . they were in shock . . . their eyes did not see . . . they were like from another world."

Rescuers kicked out windows when necessary to free people from the train cars. Passengers held the heads of the injured above the water until medical help arrived. Divers were sent into the river with acetylene torches to cut through the steel, while up to one hundred ambulances lined up at the top of the embankment. Crews came from as far away as Gettysburg, 30 miles away. Helicopters from nearby Olmsted Air Force Base hovered over the river, first using baskets to lift victims from the water into the choppers, then ferrying blankets and other supplies from the base to the victims and rescuers at the scene. The railroad company sent cranes to the site to try to lift the rail cars from the water.

A priest from St. Peter's Roman Catholic Church in Steelton was on hand to administer last rites. The scene was recorded by a reporter for the *Philadelphia Inquirer:* "The solemn intonations of the priests contrasted with the other sounds of the rescue operation—outcries of the injured, urgent commands of rescuers, wail of sirens, clatter of the helicopter ambulances." Members of a navy drill team heading to Maryland saw the accident and rushed from their bus to help. They helped free an eight-year-old boy whose leg was trapped. The boy was partially lying on top of his father, who had been killed.

A temporary morgue was set up at the Baldwin Fire Company headquarters in Steelton. In total, nineteen people were killed, including three members of one family. More than one hundred were injured, most of whom were taken to Harrisburg Hospital, where the nurses' residence was converted into an emergency ward to receive the injured. At the hospital, the disaster coordinator put out the call for doctors and nurses, and reported that 100 physicians and at least 400 nurses rushed in to help. Among the injured was a worker at the Bethlehem Steel plant. Nick Matesevac was starting out for home when he saw the cars tumble into the river, "as though a big hand just pushed them." As Matesevac was running to the scene, he tripped and fell down a steep embankment, breaking his leg.

As darkness fell, workers set up floodlights on a river barge. The last of the bodies was not recovered until after midnight. Bernard Gallagher, a major from the Olmsted base, said the scene was "as bad as anything in the war, and I mean both the Korean War and World War II. The worst part came when wives, husbands and parents began looking for their families in the crash." Other rescuers said the most haunting sight of the day was red Phillies baseball pennants floating out of the submerged cars and down the river.

Investigators would determine that a maintenance crew working that day on the tracks had not installed enough rail anchors, so the tracks were out of alignment. The engineers of the train said they saw trouble in the tracks up ahead and tried to stop in time, but it was too late. A fireman onboard a train that left Harrisburg a few hours earlier testified that he felt "a rough condition of track," but he didn't think it was serious enough to report the problem to anyone.

THE TOWN THAT'S ON FIRE

Underground Centralia Fires

Since 1962

It didn't take much to put out the fire, or so they thought. The volunteer crew that responded to the siren on a warm, sunny day in May 1962 arrived quickly at the fire in a rubbish dump on the southeast side of Centralia. They hosed down the burning trash and shoveled clay over the fire, quickly putting out the flames. Then they went back to whatever they were doing when the fire bell rang out.

But this was no ordinary trash fire. What had been used for several years as a town garbage dump was an abandoned mining pit. Underneath the surface of this central Pennsylvania town lay miles and miles of anthracite coal—and it was underground that the fire went, and where it remains to this day.

A town in Columbia County north of Harrisburg, Centralia had been around since 1841, when Jonathan Faust opened the Bull's Head Tavern. Incorporated in 1866, the village was almost universally described as a "nice little town." In its mining heyday, Centralia was home to 3,000 people; by the 1960s, the population was down to about 1,100. It was a God-fearing community, home to five churches. There wasn't much to do in Centralia, and the people who lived there liked it that way, liked a place where you could be content to raise your children and grow old. Families had lived for generations in the small homes that lined the streets. Not much changed—you could count on getting your gas at John Coddington's Amoco station, cashing your checks with Helen Womer at the local bank, and spending your Fourth of July watching the huge bonfire down the hill in Byrnesville.

The sustaining force of Centralia lay underground, in the anthracite coal—a particularly valuable type of coal found primarily in northeastern Pennsylvania. In fact, 95 percent of the anthracite in the western hemisphere comes from this part of Pennsylvania. Part of what makes anthracite unique is that is burns very slowly, releases very little smoke, and remains combustible with little or no human intervention.

And that was part of the problem. Once that underground fire got started in May 1962, it kept going. Feeding off of miles and miles of anthracite veins deep in the earth, the fire sparked and spread in areas that couldn't be seen aboveground. "These coal fires are like animals," a mining engineer said years later. "They live in holes, hide from predators like us, and want to eat all the time." Once it was discovered that the fire was still going strong, leaders of the borough of Centralia and the township in which it sat spent a month arguing about who should deal with the problem.

On July 26, authorities from the U.S. Bureau of Mines and the Pennsylvania Department of Mines and Mineral Industries visited Centralia. They later released a report, in which they stated, "It was recognized that the situation was serious and required immediate action." Meeting several days later, the government officials said it appeared that the fire was spreading rapidly; they recommended extinguishing it as soon as possible. Their suggestion was to begin excavating outward from the trash pit. Drilling, blasting, and excavating began at the end of August, but the contract didn't allow for overtime or weekend and holiday work. So when Labor Day weekend arrived, work stopped for five days.

Anthony Gaughan lived near where the excavating began and watched the progress. "They had it out when they started digging the first time, [but] they were only digging one shift a day," Gaughan said. "They should be digging three shifts a day when they're digging a mine fire. . . . They had it dug right out, at the corner of the cemetery . . . and they laid off for five days. I went down in that pit and looked at it, and I could see the fire swirling this way." The project stopped at the end of October when the contract funds ran out; Gaughan claimed they were just $50,000 short of completion. Some critics of the excavation claimed the exposure to oxygen just made the fire spread more quickly.

In late November, the Bureau of Mines came up with another idea: They would flush the fire out by drilling boreholes ahead of the fire and pouring down a mixture of wet sand, gravel, slurries of cement, and fly ash to suffocate the flames. The problem was that nobody knew exactly where the fire was, and some of those boreholes were drilled right into the flames. An inspector from the state Department of Mines and Mineral Industries said the drilling "created, like a volcano. And oh boy, when they busted, did that shake things and make a noise! It was red hot mad!" Inspectors were worried they might not have enough slurry to go around, so they told

workers not to fill all the way to the top. In addition, the boreholes were never capped, so the fire still had plenty of oxygen
to feed on. By March 1963, the government money had run out
again, with the official pronouncement from the U.S. Bureau
of Mines being that "No degree of control had been achieved."

In July, work began on the next idea; geologists drilled hundreds of boreholes to figure out exactly where the fire was, then
dug a huge containment trench to stop its progress. But the
fire had spread further than geologists thought, and again, crit-
ics complained that all the digging just resulted in improved
ventilation to fan the flames. At this point, officials were out of
ideas. The idea of flooding the area was rejected, and the solution of digging a pit "three-quarters of a mile long and deep as
a 45-story building" would have cost $660 million—more than
what the entire town was worth. Within a few months, the fire
had spread to the edge of Centralia and was knocking on the
door. As winter settled in, residents in some sections of town
were pleased that they no longer had to shovel snow; it melted
on its own. Kathy Gadinski said she was able to harvest toma-
toes at Christmas from her backyard garden.

The government tried in fits and starts to fight the fire
using boreholes and slurry over the next decade while facing
increasingly difficult political hurdles. Nothing worked. And
the residents of Centralia started to worry. People began getting headaches and feeling lightheaded in their homes. The
underground gas tanks at the local gas station were heating up.
Joan Girolami said that when contractors dug boreholes in her
backyard, they found the temperature to be 700 degrees.
Steam started spewing out of parts of Route 61, the main road
into Centralia. Water from the cold water tap ran hot in some
homes. John Coddington passed out in his sleep and had to be

Just another day in Centralia—with steam spewing out of Route 61, the community's main road. TOM RATHBUN, PENNSYLVANIA DEPARTMENT OF ENVIRONMENTAL PROTECTION

taken to the hospital, where doctors gave him oxygen. Still, the government took no action.

Then came Valentine's Day, 1981. Twelve-year-old Todd Domboski was tinkering with a motorcycle with his cousin near his grandmother's house. "I saw a little smoke a couple of yards from where we were working on the bike. So I went over and brushed away some leaves 'cause I thought someone had thrown a match and I wanted to make sure there was no fire," Domboski said later. The ground opened up beneath him. "I went down to my knees, then my waist, and just kept going. I grabbed onto some roots and was screaming for my cousin. I couldn't see him; there was smoke everywhere. I just heard him screaming, "Put your hand up! Put your hand up!" I was in over my head when he finally grabbed me." The hole, it turned out, was more than 150 feet deep and was loaded with carbon monoxide. Once the news media heard the story, the whole world learned about Centralia, Pennsylvania—the town that was on fire.

Back on the case under the glare of public scrutiny, the government installed gas detectors in houses. These black boxes sounded screeching alarms if gas fumes rose too high. The state moved a trailer in to house Department of Environmental Protection (DEP) inspectors, who became so familiar to Centralians that many would pull a chair up to the kitchen table for a cup of coffee. "Wayne and Dennis from DEP would come to check for gases every day," Sheila Klementovich said. "It became very matter-of-fact for the kids, like second nature to them." When the alarms went off, residents would open windows to air out their homes for a few hours, winter or not. Signs went up in hot spots warning about the danger. Some people complained of health problems or questioned whether the gases were to blame for their children's asthma. "People I know are getting sick from the gases, with headaches and nausea and just getting tired," Mary Gasperetti said. (A health study conducted years later by the Hershey Medical Center showed that Centralians suffered from a greater incidence of respiratory problems, hypertension, depression, and anxiety than residents in a similar town nearby.)

By this time, the flames were advancing in several directions, and the government's only idea for putting the fire out was to dig a huge trench that would basically cut the town in two. Some 1,800 boreholes with smoking pipes rising from the ground dotted the town. The Pennsylvania Emergency Management Agency relocated some of the families in the "fire zone" into temporary housing. By late 1981, the U.S. Office of Surface Mining announced, "We have no plans to fight the fire any further." James Watt, the U.S. Secretary of the Interior, said, "Our experts believe it will burn itself out. There is not a threat to health and safety."

About the same time, the Department of the Interior proposed a buyout plan for twenty-seven of the worst-affected houses. But many residents were upset—either because their homes were excluded from the buy-out or because they were being forced to relocate when they didn't want to. Grassroots efforts grew out of kitchen table discussions. Joan Girolami founded Concerned Citizens Action Group Against the Centralia Mine Fire (CCAGCMF). As its president, the group elected Thomas Larkin, who had recently returned to Centralia after twenty years. "I started to walk around the town, and I saw steam coming up," Larkin said, "pipes in the middle of the street here and steam coming up there, and I thought, 'Jeez, what the hell is going on here?'" When *People* magazine came to report on the fires, Larkin put on a chef's hat and cracked an egg into a frying pan over a fire vent; the yolk was firm in fifteen minutes. Larkin's group thought the only solution was total relocation of Centralia's residents at government expense.

But there were people equally as vehement about wanting to stay, believing the extent of the fire and its dangers had been greatly exaggerated. Reverend Anthony McGinley and Helen Womer organized Residents to Save the Borough of Centralia. Members held rallies chanting "Set Centralia Free!" while church bells rang out. Conspiracy theories surfaced along with the steam—the government and the coal companies were in cahoots, trying to get the people out of Centralia so they could mine the valuable coal below.

Relations in the once-friendly town began to fray. Former friends were shouting at each other at town meetings. "Instead of fighting the fire, they are fighting each other," one resident noted. Mary Gasperetti was a devout Catholic, but her parish priest was against residents leaving town; one Easter Sunday Gasperetti wouldn't let her family receive communion from the priest. When Helen Womer and Joan Girolami were scheduled to appear on a television show together, they refused to ride in the same limousine to the studios. Helen Womer declared, "The fire has not destroyed this community. The government has. Sensationalism by the press has. Radical elements within our community have." Girolami later said, "You know, they say small towns are so nice. Put a tragedy in a small town, you'll find out how nice it is. Put a disaster there, and it's not so nice anymore."

Many in town were convinced that if Centralia had been the site of a natural disaster—a flood or a tornado—government aid would have poured in to help. Sister Honor Murphy, a Dominican nun who helped organize a new community several miles away for Centralia exiles, said, "In a natural disaster, everyone loses their house, everybody loses everything. So you put on the boots and you pitch in and you help . . . 'cause those are human, natural disasters. But this other thing, I believe, has tended to divide people."

On August 11, 1983, the residents of Centralia held a referendum, voting 345 to 200 to accept the federal government's buyout and relocation plan. The mayor at the time, John Wondoloski, remembered, "I didn't feel good announcing the vote to a town that's a hundred and some years old and has a lot of memories." The government approved $42 million for the program, and in short order red numbers were spray-painted on houses that had been sold and marked for demolition. In December 1984, the bulldozers moved in, and in 1985, some one hundred houses were destroyed. Helen Womer was on hand on August 20, 1985, when her beloved United Methodist Church was torn down. By 1986, most of the town's homes had been condemned.

Still, some residents refused to budge. The government set a deadline, after which holdouts would no longer be able to receive government money for their homes. For the next decade, deadlines were extended, houses sold, and new deadlines were set, as the population of Centralia slowly dwindled. Some built new homes in nearby towns, while others moved across the country to be close to family. Two residents who had fought the relocation died of heart attacks while preparing to move. Upon receiving an eviction notice, a retired miner shot his wife, then drove south of town and set himself on fire in his car.

In 1992 the state of Pennsylvania took possession of Centralia's land using its power of eminent domain. Still, eighty-four people refused to move. The county government stopped cutting the grass in the town's public areas. Weeds grew to 5 feet high, attracting skunks, foxes, and other wildlife. Traffic was detoured away from Route 61 into town. And the signs went up:

WARNING—DANGER—UNDERGROUND MINE FIRE
WALKING OR DRIVING IN THIS AREA COULD RESULT
IN SERIOUS INJURY OR DEATH.
DANGEROUS GASES ARE PRESENT. GROUND IS
PRONE TO SUDDEN COLLAPSE.

In 2002 the U.S. Postal Service eliminated Centralia's zip code.

But those who stayed behind make do as best they can. They refresh the paint on a wooden heart (nailed to a tree) that says WE LOVE CENTRALIA. A retired miner unlocks the gates at the St. Ignatius cemetery every morning and locks them every evening. During Christmas they light a tree and put up a manger scene at what used to be the town's former main intersection. Tourists occasionally drive through, asking for directions to see the town that's on fire.

The truth is there's not much to see, just some occasional smoke rising from cracks in the road or the smell of sulfur on a bad day. A single slim home stands on what used to be a street of row houses. Crumbling streets lead nowhere. Fire hydrants stand ready near fields where houses once stood, obvious only by concrete steps that rise from the weeds. One reporter described "a *Twilight Zone* eeriness to this ghost town," pointing out that one of the few places where the smoke regularly rises from the ground is around the cemetery.

The remaining residents hold monthly town council meetings overseen by Mayor Lamar Mervine, who volunteered for the job when the former mayor left town in 1993. The municipal building remains padlocked. There are no children, schools, or shops. Because no one technically owns property in Centralia, no one has to pay property taxes. Every once in a while, a letter arrives from some government agency telling them they're still in danger. The 2000 census showed twenty-one people living in Centralia; by 2005, that had dwindled to twelve. Most of the remaining handful of residents say they are "too old to move." Some are hoping to hang in there until 2016, when a time capsule buried in 1966 next to the veterans' memorial will be opened. Mayor Mervine points out that the fire has been burning for forty years, yet "there's never been a casualty of any kind. . . . We've got better air here than they have in Harrisburg." Mervine still believes the fire will be doused out by eventually rolling into an underground aquifer.

The remaining residents believe the government is just waiting for the remaining few to die off, saying no politician wants to be associated with the image of old people being forcibly evicted from their homes. But living there wears you down, the residents report. One holdout said, "You watch everything you ever knew slowly being erased."

Under it all, the fire still burns. Geologists say it could continue to burn for several hundred years.

This June 23, 1972, photo shows senior citizens being rescued from their homes by boats as a business catches fire. Hurricane Agnes made the Susquehanna River overflow its banks in Wilkes-Barre, causing heavy flooding and damage along the full length of the river. AP/WORLD WIDE PHOTOS/PHIL BUTLER, SCRANTON TIMES

"AGNES REWROTE THE BOOK"

Hurricane Agnes

1972

No one paid much attention to the tropical storm forming over the Yucatan Peninsula in mid-June, 1972. The hurricane season was just beginning, and the winds of the first name-worthy storm that year—Agnes—barely even qualified the storm as a hurricane, with top winds of only 85 miles per hour. When the storm came on shore at the Florida panhandle on June 19, it downed trees and caused scattered damage, but quickly weakened. Everyone thought that was the end of Agnes. Unfortunately, it was just the beginning.

Agnes proceeded on her way over the Southeast, heading over North Carolina and out into the Atlantic Ocean on June 21. But instead of continuing on out to sea, the storm grew stronger, drawing new energy from the Atlantic's warm waters and changing her path, taking aim at the northeastern United States.

It had already been a wet June. The first two weeks had brought up to 2 inches of rain across Pennsylvania. Some areas of the state had recorded fourteen straight days of rain. Water levels in the rivers were rising and the ground was saturated, but so far no major problems had been reported. That was about to change. By the time Agnes came back on shore, her winds had strengthened to tropical storm levels, and she had combined with another low-pressure storm system. After barreling through Virginia and Maryland, Agnes came to a quick halt. The storm stagnated over Pennsylvania, and over the next two days, she would drop up to 18 inches of rain onto the soggy state below.

It was too much for the rivers to handle. Across the state, water poured over the banks of already swollen streams, flooding major cities and small towns alike, washing out bridges and roads, destroying homes and crops, and stranding hundreds of thousands of people.

The Susquehanna River had never been so high. The river takes a winding path through Pennsylvania, entering from the north at the New York border, jogging east through the small city of Wilkes-Barre, then turning southwest toward the state capital of Harrisburg before emptying into the Chesapeake Bay in Maryland. The Susquehanna had flooded before, in 1936, when it crested in Wilkes-Barre at a record 33 feet above normal levels. Concerned about future floods, the city had constructed huge dikes capable of holding back a 37-foot water rise.

No one could imagine a storm that could breach the dikes. Jim Lee, the editor of the local paper, the *Times Leader and Evening News*, was quoted as saying, "We couldn't bring ourselves to believe that the river might break through." When orders came to evacuate some residents on Thursday night, many people didn't want to leave. "People were mad. Some were still in their pajamas," a local weather reporter remembers. "They were sure the levee would hold. It [the water] had never come close to going over it."

But Agnes did send water spilling over the top of the levee, sending thousands of residents running from their homes and leaving much of Wilkes-Barre under up to 9 feet of water. The official cresting of the Susquehanna during Agnes was eventually put at 40 feet, but that is an estimate, as the flood wiped out the city's measuring equipment.

John Hope, who went on to become an expert in tropical weather for the Weather Channel, had two sisters who lived near the river in Wilkes-Barre. "They and their families had to flee for their lives in the middle of the night," Hope recalls. "Their homes were completely inundated, resulting in a complete loss of their household possessions." Hope also had a cousin who lived across the river in the town of Kingston who had to be rescued by a helicopter from the roof of her house. Boats and helicopters rescued thousands of stranded people in the area. There were 6,600 homes in Kingston, and only 20 were above water at the height of the flooding.

In Wilkes-Barre and the surrounding Wyoming Valley, a total of 13,000 people lost their homes. "Houses were underwater—hundreds of them just gone," said a reporter on the scene. "People were wandering through the streets. Mud was hanging off the ceilings. Nothing was salvageable. People were even throwing out wedding pictures. The odor was horrible." Downed wires started numerous fires that were left to burn since fire trucks couldn't reach them. Three hospitals had to be evacuated. Staff at several radio stations broadcasting emergency information had to quickly leave their studios as the waters moved in. Though police tried to maintain control, there were reports of looting in the business district. And residents were confronted with the gruesome sight of caskets floating in the floodwaters near a historic graveyard.

One hundred miles downstream at Harrisburg, the situation was equally as bleak, as the Susquehanna pushed more than a half-mile out of its banks, virtually cutting off the city. The airport was under water, and all major roads into the city were blocked. Streets in the downtown area of the capitol were under several feet of water, and the flooding even pushed into the governor's mansion, which had to be evacuated by boat at 3:30 A.M. The Georgian-style mansion had been completed just four years earlier at a cost of $2.4 million. Now, the entire first floor was covered with water and mud, as workers hurried to move antiques and artwork to the second floor. "We'll stay somewhere," said Governor Milton Shapp. "With the devastation we have here in Pennsylvania, there's no time to worry about the mansion." The governor called out the National Guard to help with evacuations in Harrisburg and throughout the state. (It was the largest state activation of the National Guard until 2005, when 2,500 troops were mobilized and sent to the Gulf Coast to help with the cleanup from Hurricane Katrina.)

Northwest of Harrisburg in State College, Pennsylvania State University had to cancel its graduation ceremonies because so many roads in the area were impassable. Though the university did have a small ceremony for people still on campus, it urged others not to try to come, saying the area was "virtually unreachable."

In downtown Pittsburgh, which lies at the convergence of three rivers, the mayor asked all businesses to move their employees out once the waters started to rise. Businesses pulled down their steel flood doors, and sandbags prevented most serious flooding.

The Philadelphia area reported receiving only 4 to 5 inches of rain from Agnes, but even still, the storm caused major problems. The Schuylkill River drains from some of the hardest-hit areas, and its levels rose to record levels. Many areas along the river reported water so deep that cars were floating. In Pottstown, 35 miles west of Philadelphia, the Schuylkill crested 8 feet above flood levels. The town was described as being entirely cut off. Some residents were forced to climb on their roofs to escape the floodwaters, and navy helicopters were sent in to rescue them. Waters from the flood also inundated a Pottstown site where used oil was stored, resulting in an estimated six million gallons of oil being washed into the waters of the Schuylkill.

Across the state, 220,000 people were left homeless by Hurricane Agnes, and forty-eight people lost their lives in the storm. Among the dead were thirty-two-year-old Samuel Kauffman and his ten-month-old son. A member of Lancaster County's Amish community, Kauffman and his son were drowned after their horse-drawn buggy was swept into a swift creek. (In addition, though not counted in the storm's casualties, a television helicopter covering the floods near Harrisburg crashed, killing all four people onboard.) The storm caused $2.1 billion in damage (in 1972 dollars), making it the state's costliest natural disaster on record. After taking a helicopter tour over Pennsylvania, President Richard Nixon declared the entire state a disaster area. A chief of the National Weather Service later said, "Agnes rewrote the book on inland flooding and the impact a tropical storm can have hundreds of miles from the coast."

A DEADLY MYSTERY

Legionnaire's Disease Outbreak
1976

Philadelphia was breathing a sigh of relief in late July 1976. After years of preparations, the city had put its best face forward for the celebration of the country's bicentennial. President Gerald Ford had led a host of dignitaries at Independence Hall ceremonies on July 4. With no major glitches, the worst that was said about the bicentennial events was that they were a bit dull. The city was now hoping to reap the tourism benefits from the celebration and relax for the rest of the summer.

Among those filling the city's hotels that July were thousands of members of the American Legion, in town for the fifty-eighth annual state convention of the American Legion Department of Pennsylvania. The official proceedings were being held at the Bellevue-Stratford Hotel, the so-called "Grande Dame of Broad Street." Built over two years at a cost of $8 million (in 1904 dollars), the elegant Bellevue-Stratford had been described at that time as the most luxurious hotel in the country. The convention was held from July 21 to July 24, with some members tacking on a few days to enjoy the city with their families. By all appearances, the gathering was a success.

But a few days after the convention ended, some who had attended began to get sick. Just three days after returning to his small Pennsylvania town, retired Air Force Captain Raymond Brennan was dead. The next day a second man who had been at the convention died outside of Pittsburgh. By the beginning of August, seventeen people were dead, and dozens of Legionnaires were sick with the same flu-like symptoms: fever, chills, coughing, and body aches.

Charles Mike, a retired letter carrier, got sick on the bus on the way home to Wilkes-Barre. He spent thirty days in a hospital, near death, packed in ice and fighting a sky-high fever. Mike's friend Russell Dugan also became ill and lay comatose in a hospital for two weeks. He said doctors had no idea what was wrong and were drawing blood samples from him every fifteen minutes and racing them to a lab.

American Legion volunteers Dorothy Cusick and Alice Cherubin accompanied their husbands on the trip and took their kids along. "The convention was a vacation for a lot of the families," Cusick said later. "After we returned home, we started hearing about people getting sick and dying."

Michael Dolan had shared a room in Philadelphia with his cousin, Jimmy, and his friend Ralph, who both died shortly after returning home. They were among the youngest victims, and Michael Dolan said it was their deaths that made the Legion say, "This is hitting our Legionnaires."

Mario Maloberti thought he had a case of the flu when he returned to Jeannette, Pennsylvania. He was coughing and had a fever, but he wasn't that concerned until he heard that other Legionnaires had gotten sick and that some had died. He went to the hospital, where he stayed for nine days. "I watched the funerals on the TV in the hospital," Maloberti later told a Pittsburgh reporter. One of his neighbors and a fellow veteran, Louis Byerly, died while Maloberti was in the hospital.

Maloberti credits Edward Hoak with connecting the dots. The adjutant of the Pennsylvania American Legion, Hoak had begun receiving many reports of men getting sick and dying, and he realized they everyone affected had attended the convention in Philadelphia. He was the first to sound the alarm, notifying the Pennsylvania Department of Health and local reporters. Almost immediately, panic set in. The headline in the *Philadelphia Inquirer* on August 3 screamed: "Mysterious Disease Kills 16 Who Attended Meeting Here." By the next day, the headline read "Mystery Death Toll Reaches 20." Within a month, twenty-nine people linked to the convention were dead, and more than 200 others were sick.

Dorothy Cusick had been elected president of the American Legion Auxiliary Department of Pennsylvania at the convention. "I started my year as president by going to funerals and visiting the sick," she remembered. Not only were people afraid, but those who had been in Philadelphia faced another problem. "When we got back home, people were treating us so rotten," Cusick told a reporter. Her friend Alice Cherubin agreed. "When I went to stores in Beechview, everybody knew I'm with the Legion," she said. "They didn't want to touch any of my money or nothing. They thought I was contagious."

John Titus had been a delegate at the convention and he said neighbors were reluctant to have contact with anyone who had been there. "My washing machine broke down and I called Sears for maintenance," he recalled. "The man knew I had been at the convention and he refused to come in and fix my machine until the next week." Mario Maloberti's wife, Janet, said it got so bad that she had to shout to people on the street. "I was losing my voice because nobody would come near me," Maloberti recounted. Most doctors insisted that the mystery illness was not contagious, but still, no one knew what the sickness was or what was causing it.

Joseph Adams had been elected state commander at the convention. "I went to about fifteen or so funerals in about twelve days," he remembered years later. "I drove close to 65,000 miles that year, meeting with people who had some kind of theory."

And it seemed as though everyone had a theory about what was causing what came to be known as Legionnaire's Disease. People were terrified that the illnesses signaled the beginning of a swine flu epidemic, which was a major problem that year in Asia. Many thought a mysterious virus was to blame. Some favored the "trash fever" theory that the illness was caused by something in the garbage that had piled up in Philadelphia during a month-long slowdown by sanitation workers. Others thought a communist plot and poison were involved. Someone even questioned whether the blame might lie with the pretzels that conventioneers had snacked on in the city's bars.

Ted Tsai was among the first people sent to Philadelphia by the U.S. Centers for Disease Control to act as a disease detective. He and his team set up headquarters at the Bellevue-Stratford, which by then had virtually no other customers. Years later he told a reporter he received a call from a man who had attended a magicians' convention at the hotel before the Legionnaires came to town. This man was afraid he had caused the outbreak by setting off a smoke bomb in the Bellevue's ventilation system. "This guy was just tortured and had to get it off his chest," Tsai said.

The Bellevue-Stratford Hotel never recovered from the bad publicity of being asso-
ciated with Legionnaire's Disease, at least not until it was reinvented as a luxury
hotel in 2002. LIBRARY OF CONGRESS, PHOTO BY JACK BOUCHER, 1976

More realistically, Tsai said there was much suspicion about the hotel's air-conditioning system. Epidemiologists fanned out across the city, collecting samples of water, food, dirt, bugs, and dozens of other possible culprits. Then on January 18, 1977, scientists at the Centers for Disease Control in Atlanta announced they had figured out the cause: a previously unknown rod-shaped bacterium, later named *Legionella pneumophila*. Researchers also announced they had developed a simple blood test that could help diagnose cases of Legionnaire's Disease.

It would take years of debate for the scientific community to come to the consensus that the bacteria was spread through water droplets in the air, perhaps through the hotel's air-conditioning system. The discovery of *Legionella pneumophila* actually helped doctors solve several other medical mysteries, as it was named the probable cause of similar but less severe epidemics several years earlier at St. Elizabeth's Hospital in Washington, D.C.; at an office building in Pontiac, Michigan; and at yet another Philadelphia convention—a 1974 gathering of the Independent Association of Odd Fellows. Doctors believed that many people who had been diagnosed with pneumonia over the years had likely suffered from Legionnaire's Disease instead. Thousands of cases of the illness are now reported every year and are usually easily treated with a combination of antibiotics.

One uncounted victim of the panic that summer of the 1976 was the Bellevue-Stratford Hotel. Despite its glorious past, the hotel never recovered from the bad publicity caused by the mysterious illness. In July 1978, two years after the breakout, the Legionnaires were once again holding their annual convention in Philadelphia, and some of those attending went to visit the Bellevue, only to find that it was holding a public sale of its contents. The doors of the Bellevue remained shut for two years. After two decades and several incarnations, the Grande Dame of Broad Street reopened in 2002, housing a luxury hotel with high-end retail shops and a gourmet food court on the ground floors.

For years, many Legionnaires resented the name of their organization being associated with the medical mystery that has been called "one of the most baffling epidemics in the annals of epidemiology." "It didn't make it look too good for the American Legion because people didn't want to affiliate with us," Mario Maloberti recalled. Dorothy Cusick, the former auxiliary president, said for a time it cast a dark cloud over the group. But years later, Cusick grew to see it differently. Referring to those who died, she said, "Now I think the name is more in their memory and their honor."

"THIS IS THE BIGGIE"

Three Mile Island

1979

The 1970s found America confronting an energy crisis, with oil in short supply. By the end of the decade, the price of a barrel of oil had risen from $3.00 a barrel to $30.00 a barrel in just seven years. There was a desperate need for more affordable energy options, and to many, it appeared that the answer lay in nuclear power, a relatively cheap way of extracting power from nuclear reactions. Utilities jumped on the nuclear bandwagon, ordering the construction of dozens of nuclear power plants across the country. But the early boom in plant construction was not met with an equal effort in regulation. The still-new Nuclear Regulatory Commission (NRC) was overwhelmed. "We used to talk about inviting people in off the street to see if they didn't want to come work for the NRC, because we really had more work than we could handle," said Harold Denton, director of the NRC's Division of Nuclear Reactor Regulation in the 1970s. In fact, there was talk among some within the NRC that the organization was not paying enough attention to safety issues.

The Three Mile Island nuclear power plant was constructed on a sandbar in the middle of the Susquehanna River,
10 miles downriver from the state capital of Harrisburg. Its
Unit 2 reactor, considered state of the art, went online and
began pumping out electricity in December 1978. People in
the area had grown accustomed to the huge concrete cooling
towers belching steam, a sight easily visible from where the
busy Pennsylvania Turnpike crossed the Susquehanna. It was
the cooling towers that first signaled to the outside world that
something was wrong at Three Mile Island on March 28, 1979,
when the traffic reporter for a local Top 40 radio station called
in from his car. "Our traffic reporter was driving around and he
says, 'You know, I'm getting things up on the scanners here . . .
apparently they're mobilizing some fire equipment and emergency people at Three Mile Island,'" recalled Mike Pintek, then
news director of WKBO. "And he said, 'Oh, by the way, there's
no steam coming out of the cooling towers.'"

Just before 4:00 that morning, workers inside the plant
had been dealing with what was essentially a plumbing problem—a clogged tank, not an unusual occurrence at Three Mile
Island. But a confounding series of technical failures and
human errors over the next several days would lead to the
brink of a nuclear disaster.

When water started leaking into air lines, the valves in the
feedwater system slammed shut, including the pumps supplying water to the Unit 2 reactor. With no water, the steam gen-
erators couldn't remove heat, so—as designed—the plant's
safety system automatically shut down the steam turbine and
the reactor. This caused an immediate increase in pressure in
the nuclear reactor. Again, as designed, a safety relief valve
opened to relieve the pressure.

One of the first public indicators of the crisis came from a traffic reporter
for local radio who noticed that emergency personnel were assembling at Three
Mile Island and that steam was no longer coming out of the cooling towers.
COURTESY DEPARTMENT OF ENERGY

But then things started to go wrong. The valve was designed to close after the pressure had lowered to safe levels, but it malfunctioned and remained open, allowing cooling water to drain out. (There had been eleven previous reports of similar valve malfunctions at other nuclear plants.) As the core of the reactor began to overheat, the crew in the Three Mile Island control room had no idea the valve was stuck open. With alarms ringing and lights flashing, the operators were confused by some of the contradictory readings they were getting from their monitoring equipment. Believing the valve was closed and there was adequate coolant in the core, they made the decision to shut off the emergency water system. The nuclear core began to overheat once again.

"If the operators had not intervened in that accident at Three Mile Island and shut off the pumps, the plant would have saved itself," Mike Gray, an engineer and journalist, said in a public television documentary. "They had thought of absolutely everything except what would happen if the operators intervened anyway. So the operators thought they were saving the plant by cutting off the emergency water when, in fact, they had just sealed its fate."

According to one operator in the control room, the console then "lit up like a Christmas tree," as the sound of alarms filled the room. Though the crew was well trained in nuclear technology, they struggled to keep up with a confusing onslaught of computer printouts and contradictory information. "There was such an avalanche of alarms that the operators couldn't really address any of those on a real-time basis," said Jim Higgins of the NRC. "They were just catching up and trying to prioritize and handle the most important ones and do what they could." As far as the operators were concerned, the reactor's core was still covered in coolant and safe. In reality, temperatures in the reactor were soaring. By early morning, the temperatures in the core were at 4,300 degrees, just 900 degrees away from meltdown.

At 6:15 A.M., with the control room now crowded with people, an alarm sounded: "Radiation in the control room." Contaminated water had leaked into an adjoining building, releasing radioactive gas. The operators donned emergency respirators. It was at this point that Supervisor Gary Miller decided he had to declare a general emergency, the first ever at a nuclear power plant in the United States. By definition, a general emergency meant there was the "potential for serious radiological consequences to the health and safety of the general public." William Dornsife, a nuclear engineer employed by the state Department of Environmental Resources, was on the phone with the control room when he heard a background announce-ment that parts of the plant should be evacuated. Dornsife remembers thinking at that moment, "This is the biggie."

Once he got the call from his traffic reporter, radio journal-ist Mike Pintek put in a call to Three Mile Island, where the harried telephone operator patched his call right into the con-trol room. "I hear all this commotion . . . in the background," Pintek said. "There's a guy on the line. I tell him who I am, and I ask him, is there fire equipment there? And he says, 'I can't talk now, we've got a problem.'" Pintek did a report on the air at 8:25 A.M., and word about trouble at Three Mile Island began to spread quickly.

At about the same time, Pennsylvania Governor Richard Thornburgh was told about the situation by aides. "The minute I heard that there had been an accident at a nuclear facility, I knew we were in another dimension," Thornburgh said in the PBS documentary. Thornburgh called upon his lieutenant gov-ernor, William Scranton, who headed the state's emergency council. "There had never been anything like this . . . it wasn't something you could see or feel or taste or touch," Scranton recalled. "We were talking about radiation, which generated an enormous amount of fear." Still, having been reassured by Metropolitan Edison, Three Mile Island's owner, that no radia-tion had been detected outside of the plant, Scranton held a press conference saying there was no public danger.

That sense of confidence soon evaporated, however. "What I had said in the morning was, 'There has been no significant offsite release,' only to find out moments later that, in fact, there had been an offsite release," Scranton recalled. "The indignation that welled up within me was memorable. . . . It was at that point that I realized that we could not rely on

Metropolitan Edison for the kind of information we needed to make decisions."

As reporters began to descend, Metropolitan Edison realized it had a serious public relations crisis and appointed an engineer, Jack Herbein, as spokesperson. Herbein had no experience with the media, however, and both the media and some government leaders quickly became frustrated with his lack of information. "If you had gone home from that first press conference, you would have presumed that the problem would have been cleaned up overnight," reporter Gene Schenck recalled. Robert Reid, the mayor of nearby Middletown, wasn't satisfied with the answers he was getting from Herbein either. "When I asked him about the release and the time of the accident, he more or less looked at it from the standpoint of, 'Mayor, you don't know anything about nuclear energy. I'm the expert,'" Reid said. "I was upset with the way things were being handled and the way we were lied to."

With the control room at Three Mile Island still in chaos, the NRC set up an emergency center in Bethesda, Maryland, and sent several inspectors to Pennsylvania. Those employees were astounded at what greeted them. "As we were walking through the turbine building, which was basically like a ghost town . . . we saw these two other people from the plant wearing their anticontamination radiation suits, and they also had their respirator masks on," NRC inspector Jim Higgins said. "It gave the impression like, there is something very wrong here." Higgins recalled that everyone in the control room was also wearing respirators, which made communication difficult and critical telephone conversations muffled.

Adding to the tense atmosphere was the fact that there were only two telephone lines into the control room, and anyone trying to call in got a busy signal. That included Babcock & Wilcox, the Virginia-based designers of the reactor, who had trouble reaching someone in the control room with the urgent message to get water moving through the core immediately. Once the water was turned back on, the temperature in the reactor began to fall, and everyone breathed a sigh of relief. On the evening news that night, the message was one of reassurance. "It was the first step in a nuclear nightmare—as far as we know at this hour, no worse than that," intoned Walter Cronkite. "There was no apparent serious contamination of workers."

Thursday morning, despite assurances that the danger had passed, Lieutenant Governor Scranton felt the need for a first-hand assessment of the situation at Three Mile Island. He later recalled, "Being thirty years old and maybe thinking I was more immortal than I really was, I said, 'I'm going to go down there.'"

When he arrived, Scranton was given protective gear to put on. "It took me 45 minutes to get in all of the suits and putting all of the dosimeters on me so that they knew how much radiation that I got," he said. "I remember walking in there, and I must say I was quite unnerved the closer I got to it. When I started walking in . . . I looked down and I saw on the floor this water, which looked like water in your basement except it happened to be in the auxiliary building of a nuclear power plant. I realized that what was around me was highly contaminated." Scranton was reassured, though, when he left two-and-a-half hours later and reported to Governor Thornburgh that everything was under control.

But just twenty-four hours later, the crisis and the chaos returned in full force. There were reports that a burst of

radioactive gas had escaped from Three Mile Island, and a call
came into the Governor's office from the NRC with the recom-
mendation to evacuate the area around the plant. No one
seemed to know what was really going on. In Washington
Joseph Hendrie, the chairman of the NRC, told an aide,
"Thornburgh's information is ambiguous, mine is nonexist-
ent. We're like a couple of blind men trying to make a decision." The governor was uneasy, to say the least, about the
state's ability to handle a large evacuation. He had earlier asked
an assistant to look over the current emergency plans. "His
report to me was chilling," Thornburgh recalled. "One of the
things I'll never forget was that he said that under the regimen
that had been established by the counties on either side of the
river, one Dauphin County where Harrisburg was, and Cum-
berland County, across the river, that their evacuees would
meet head-on in the middle of the bridge over which they were
to be evacuated."

The atmosphere became even more charged when during
the morning, sirens started blaring as someone set off Harrisburg's civil defense alarm. There was no immediate danger,
but the mistake further rattled the nerves of people living in
the area. Even though Thornburgh shortly received word that
the amount of radiation released had been hugely overesti-
mated, a sense of disorder was growing. And more and more
journalists were filing into town.

One of those journalists was Mike Gray, a reporter who had
also written the script for the just-released movie, *The China
Syndrome*, which depicted a near meltdown at a nuclear power
plant. For Gray, the confluence of events was surreal. "At one
of the major New York dailies the managing editor stood up on
his desk and shouted, 'Who here has seen *The China Syn-*

drome?' Gray said. "Three guys raised their hand and he said, 'You, you, you, you're goin' to Harrisburg.' So the movie then became a briefing film for the press."

And the media was losing its patience with Metropolitan Edison. Jack Herbein said in an 11 A.M. press conference on Friday that "The release that was made yesterday was within the limits that were acceptable. . . . I don't know why we need to tell you each and every thing that we do." To which radio reporter Mike Pintek replied, "Well, why not, Jack? You know, we only live here, and you may kill us here before you're all finished."

Though the amount of radiation released on Friday was less than originally reported, Governor Thornburgh got a disturbing call from the NRC chairman late that morning, recommending a limited evacuation of people at risk living near the power plant. His worst fears were being realized. At a quickly arranged news conference, Thornburgh urged all pregnant women and preschool-age children within a 5-mile radius of Three Mile Island to leave the area. Sound trucks drove slowly through communities, broadcasting the news. The panic throughout the area escalated even further.

"People left their jobs, came home, packed their cars and their children," recalled Middletown Mayor Robert Reid. "I remember standing on the corner and cars zipping past me and people hollering out the window, 'Watch the town.' And I said, 'Well, here I am standing here. I'm in as much danger as they are and they're leaving town and telling me to watch their homes.' Things were starting to get a little hectic."

For Marsha McHenry, it was clear that the situation was getting out of hand. "Our neighbors told me . . . that I was to come down to their house. They had guns and they had a

chainsaw and a big truck and they would get up on the high-
way, cut down any barriers that were there and fight their way
through," McHenry said. "So the idea that there was going to
be any kind of an orderly evacuation was pure fantasy." On the
way out of town, McHenry feared the worst, that the beautiful
countryside around her home would be destroyed. "It would be
so contaminated that nobody could be there for hundreds of
years," she feared. "I looked as hard as I could at everything,
and tried to burn it into my mind, what everything looked like,
because I wasn't going to see it again."

Over the next several days, 140,000 people fled the area.
"It's frightening when you see helicopters taking samples of
the air over your house," Jack Tighe told a Philadelphia
reporter. "You feel like you're sitting in the middle of a disaster
movie."

With his frustration growing, Governor Thornburgh
appealed to President Jimmy Carter to send help. Thornburgh
needed someone he could trust. As NRC official Harold Denton left for Harrisburg, he said he felt like a fireman rushing to
the scene of a fire. But Denton's presence seemed to immediately calm the situation. The governor's staff and the media
alike said they felt like there was finally someone on the scene
they could trust.

But even as Denton assured the public there was no immediate danger, a new problem was brewing inside the Unit 2
reactor: There appeared to be a hydrogen gas bubble forming
over the core, which could stop the cooling process. Once
again, there were fears of a meltdown.

Senior NRC Engineer Roger Mattson contacted Chairman
Hendrie. "What I told 'em was that we had a reactor that was
in a condition that no one had anticipated, that the core was

severely damaged," Mattson said. "I think I called it a 'horse race.'" Mattson argued for widening the evacuation.

Leading off the evening news, Walter Cronkite was much less reassuring that Friday than he had been two days earlier. "The world has never known a day quite like today," Cronkite began. "It faced the considerable uncertainties and dangers of the worst nuclear power plant accident of the atomic age. And the horror tonight is that it could get much worse. The potential is there for the ultimate risk of a meltdown at the Three Mile Island, atomic power plant outside Harrisburg, Pennsylvania."

It was hard to imagine that on Saturday morning the situation looked even more dire, but it did. Some nuclear physicists were warning NRC Chairman Hendrie that the hydrogen bubble inside Unit 2 could mix with oxygen, causing a huge explosion. Other experts said that there was no danger of an explosion whatsoever. In the Pennsylvania statehouse, confusion reigned. "We were making plans for the evacuation of not only people, but of government, of how we were going to govern in the case of the massive meltdown and escape of radioactivity," said Lieutenant Governor Scranton. "We were going through some very tough scenarios . . . and these were tired, overworked, very stressed people."

Harold Denton was remaining calm in his office near Three Mile Island, trying to bridge the gap between the very divergent predictions of an explosion. But by late that night, word of a possible explosion had leaked to the press, and hysteria was in the air. Journalist Mike Gray was on hand when Denton held an 11 P.M. news conference. "In the state capital were several hundred reporters who got the word that this thing may explode and it's . . . a stone's throw down the river from where they're standing right at this moment," Gray recalled. "They went into the press room and they weren't after a story. What they wanted to know was, 'Is it time to get out?'" It was a critical moment for radio journalist Mike Pintek. "It's Saturday night. I'm saying to myself, 'My life, at about 27 years old, is going to be over, because these arrogant utility operators have allowed this thing to run out of control and they're going to kill us,'" Pintek said.

But Harold Denton had confidence in his people on the site, and they were optimistic. At the press conference, Denton told reporters, "It's certainly days before flammability limits would be reached and many more days after that before detonation limits would be reached, all of which assume that we did nothing but sit on our hands here instead of getting the hydrogen out of the vessel." Governor Thornburgh had even more reassuring news: President Carter would visit Three Mile Island the next day. "I think this is an important vote of confidence and a further refutation of the kind of alarmist reaction that has set in in some quarters," Thornburgh said. A nuclear engineer by training, the President certainly understood what was at stake, and though some in Washington were against the visit, Carter's presence proved to be a turning point in the crisis.

One of those arguing for calm was Victor Stello, a respected engineer with the NRC who had been in touch with top nuclear physicists. But when an exhausted Stello went to mass Sunday morning, the mood was far from calm. Stello recalled, "This priest gets up and said that because of the potential for us being killed from Three Mile Island, we're going to have general absolution," a Catholic sacrament reserved for situations where death is imminent. "It was a very difficult and emotional kind of a thing . . . we had frightened them so bad they thought they were gonna die."

Still extremely wary of conditions inside the reactor, Senior Engineer Roger Mattson rushed to Harrisburg from Washington to be there when President Carter arrived. At the airport, he encountered Denton and Stello. "Here comes Roger Mattson into the hangar and here's Victor Stello, the other top NRC expert, and Stello says, 'Mattson, you son-of-a-bitch! How could you be spreading these rumors around about this hydrogen bubble,'" journalist Mike Gray said. "And Mattson is saying, 'Victor, that bubble is ready to explode and if you can't see that, you're crazy.' And they're screaming back and forth at each other inside this hangar. This had to be a fairly thrilling moment for Harold Denton as the President's deputy, because here is the President, the chief executive, due to arrive at any moment with his wife. And here are his two top technical experts slugging it out there in the hangar over whether or not this place was about to blow up."

When President Carter and his wife, Rosalynn, helicoptered in, Denton briefed them on the situation. As writer Dan Martin later explained, Carter felt he had no choice. "What is he to do? If he turns around and walks away after he's come up here in order to calm the public down, that message is unmistakable. And so he did the only thing he felt he could." As Carter's motorcade traveled to the plant, people who had stayed behind stood by the side of the road and cheered.

At the same time, Victor Stello and Roger Mattson continued to pour over data about the explosion theory. Finally, Stello realized there was a flaw in Mattson's calculations. In fact, there was not a threat that the hydrogen bubble would explode; it had been a false alarm.

The image of President Carter and his wife inside Three Mile Island—broadcast around the world—effectively brought an end to the crisis. "A lot of people felt that if the president is coming here and bringing his wife, things must be all right," Robert Reid said. Reassured of their safety, people in the area began to return to their homes. The government trucked in lead bricks to build a protective wall around the reactor, and slowly but surely, the hydrogen was released from the system. Unit 2 was shut down for good a month after the accident began. The last venting of gases occurred in 1981, but the cleanup took close to twelve years and cost nearly $1 billion. Three Mile Island's Unit 1 stayed down for almost five years.

It would be three years before a clear picture emerged of what had happened inside the reactor. Supervising Engineer Bob Long remembered the day they finally lowered a camera into the core. "You hear the voice of the mechanic who's lowering it saying, 'One foot, two foot, we're now two feet into the core, we're now approaching three feet.' As I'm watching the tape my stomach churns more and 'Five foot. Got something.' That recognition for the first time, five feet of the core was gone. That's when we really saw that the core had been severely damaged."

"Within the NRC, no one really thought that you could have a core meltdown," Harold Denton later said. "We actually thought the plant was too well designed to have a serious accident. It was kind of like the *Titanic*."

The country's confidence in nuclear power would never recover. Though the government instituted stringent new safety standards, the damage had been done. Since the accident at Three Mile Island, not one new nuclear power plant has gone online in the United States. And since 1979, nearly one-fifth of the country's reactors have shut down. However, Three Mile Island's Unit 1 continues to operate, generating enough electricity for 300,000 homes. Though many still question the long-term health effects for those living near Three Mile Island, the official government line is that the release of radiation "had negligible effects on the physical health of individuals or the environment."

Looking back on the accident years later, Governor Thornburgh said, "I don't see how you could ever erase the memories of frustration, of uncertainty . . . punctuated by moments of stark terror that attach to an incident like Three Mile Island . . . and the eternal sense of relief and deliverance when that was finally over."

"A TORNADO COCKTAIL"

Tornado Outbreak
1985

In any given year, an average of seven category F4 tornadoes touch down somewhere in the United States. The second strongest on the Fujita scale that meteorologists use to measure storm intensity, F4s are described as "devastating" tornadoes with winds between 207 and 260 miles per hour. On a single day in 1985, a total of seven F4s hit northwest Pennsylvania. Still rarer, even in the Midwest's "tornado alley," is an F5 tornado, classified as an "incredible" storm, with winds of up to 318 mph. Only once in recorded history has an F5 tornado touched down in Pennsylvania. It happened on the same day that the F4s touched down—May 31, 1985—the ninety-sixth anniversary of the Johnstown Flood.

That Friday morning, forecasters were monitoring several weather systems nationwide. Texas was having some nasty weather, with the possibility of tornadoes developing. Watching the morning news from her home in Albion, Pennsylvania, Linda Quay was feeding her children breakfast. "Aren't you glad we don't live in Texas and don't have to worry about a tornado?" she asked her kids. As far as Linda was concerned, her

biggest weather concern was a chance of thunderstorms forecast later in the day for the Great Lakes and Upper Ohio Valley
eastward. That meant her son's T-ball game that evening might
be rained out.

The older kids in Wheatland, some 70 miles south of
Albion, had graduated from T-ball to Little League. Dave
Kostka was onboard to umpire a game that night. The thirty-
six-year-old postal carrier had just returned from his honeymoon several weeks earlier; he was looking forward to another
season overseeing the diamond.

Midmorning, the meteorologists at the National Weather
Service in Erie received a warning from the National Severe
Storms Forecast Center in Kansas City about the possibility of
severe thunderstorms developing in their region. A cold air
mass that had dumped snow in Colorado and Wyoming was
producing high winds and dust storms in Nebraska. It was
looking increasingly possible that this cold front would collide
with a band of unstable weather that had caused the record
heat in Texas and spawned tornadoes in Missouri and Iowa.
The warning out of Kansas City indicated the two systems
would meet south of the Great Lakes and could cause problems. One meteorologist later described the confluence of
storm systems that day as a "tornado cocktail." But as the day
progressed, the radar screens around the area remained quiet,
so meteorologists were not surprised when the National Severe
Storms Forecast Center downgraded the warning for severe
thunderstorms to "slight" in the early afternoon. It looked like
everyone was going to get off easy.

Gene Hart wasn't so sure. The assistant park superintendent of Pymatuning State Park on the Ohio-Pennsylvania border, Hart had heard the forecast about the possibility of severe

weather. As the campers, boaters, and picnickers gathered in the park that day, the skies did not seem threatening. But Hart would later say he had an uneasy feeling about the weather, though he couldn't quite figure out why. As the afternoon wore on, it became increasingly obvious that his uneasiness was warranted.

By midafternoon, severe thunderstorms were pounding the region of Ontario north of Lake Erie. At about 4 P.M., the computer screens in Kansas City lit up with activity along the Ohio border, and the conditions were suddenly ripe for tornadoes. Meteorologist Steve Weiss issued an alert over the Centralized Storm Information System: "BULLETIN—IMMEDIATE BROADCAST REQUESTED . . . The National Severe Storms Forecast Center has issued a tornado watch for portions of Eastern Ohio, portions of the Northern Panhandle, W. VA, portions of Western Pennsylvania . . . from 5:00 P.M. EDT until 11:00 P.M. this Friday afternoon and evening . . . Tornadoes . . . Large Hail . . . Dangerous Lightning and Damaging Thunderstorm Winds are possible in these areas."

A tornado watch was as strong as the weather alerts could get until someone had proof of tornadoes in the area. At that time, the National Weather Service used radar systems that covered 140 miles, looking for signs of the tell-tale circular storm motion. But without a confirmed report from the ground, there was no basis to issue a stronger tornado warning. The service relied on storm spotters in the so-called Skywarn Network to be their eyes in the outside world. Richard Bomboy was one of those spotters. Although confined to a wheelchair, Richard used a rotating video camera mounted on a tower at his home to monitor the weather. At 5:05 P.M., Bomboy put in a call to the National Weather Service at Erie. "Just spotted a tornado touch down . . . about 5 miles west of

Albion," he reported. "Actually, I see at least two of 'em form-ing . . . heading directly toward Albion."

A warning was issued right away, but by then, it was hardly necessary.

Roger Seeley, a volunteer fireman in Albion, was standing in front of the station when he started getting hit by hail. Look-ing up, he saw what he thought was a large flock of birds fly-ing in a circle. Then he realized it wasn't birds but debris swirling around. A thirteen-year-old girl named Tracy Petrilla was walking home across a nearby field when she saw the same thing coming right at her. Petrilla dove into a culvert to avoid being hit by debris; she later said she saw the twister divide into two parts, one passing on each side of her, then come together again as it headed right at Albion.

Pennsylvania State Trooper Bradley Mills was in his home in Albion watching television when he saw a tornado warning move across the bottom of his TV screen. Heading to a win-dow, he saw a windy, dark scene outside. Then came a knock at his door. A boy had run to the nearest house for safety. He was crying and said "Albion's blown up! It's just blown up!" Mills scanner went off about the same time, but when he went to pick up the phone, the lines were dead.

Linda Quay was relieved that her son's T-ball game had been cancelled. Now she could have dinner with her husband, Albion's assistant fire chief. But as Linda was cooking her had-dock, her husband's CB radio signaled a message calling all firemen to report to duty. As she put her baby in the high chair and called her other children to the supper table, she noticed the family dog was whimpering and acting very strange.

Sandra Stahlsmith was also getting ready for dinner when she looked out her window to see her sons Zachary and Luke trying to catch the hail that had suddenly started to fall. She called them inside just as the fire siren went off, grabbed her baby out of his crib, and yelled for her daughters to come downstairs to the basement.

Many of the people in Albion that day would use the same words to describe the tornadoes that destroyed their community: It sounded like the roar of a freight train or jet engines heading right for them. Bob McClymond heard the roar and yelled for his wife. As they ran for the basement, Bob saw a huge branch fly by, and the plants on his kitchen windowsill were sucked out the window. Then noticing a sudden stillness, McClymond looked out his window. He said later it was as if Jackson Street had disappeared. The houses across the street were just piles of rubble, and he could hear several voices from those piles calling for help. Albion firefighter Jim Ticknor told a reporter the tornado "would come down, then lift up and hop to a different area, then it would start all over again. It just leapfrogged through town."

Linda Quay saw the trees bending outside and heard the roar. She was hurrying her children from the dinner table into the basement just as the windows blew out, sending flying glass through the room. She crawled across the broken glass to get her baby out of her high chair and huddled with her children in the basement until the silence returned. "After the glass stopped flying around, I crawled over to her," she told a reporter for the *New York Times*. "She wasn't hurt, and she wasn't even crying." One of Quay's neighbors, Eileen Hosey, said "Our neighbor's house is in my backyard, my Pontiac is at the medical center across the way, and two cars from the medical center are in my yard."

Sandra Stahlsmith had crowded her children into the fruit cellar along the only wall without a window, pulling a table

close to protect them. When the tornado hit, the house collapsed into the cellar. The wall behind her came crashing
down, pushing Sandra and her son, Luke, hard into the table.
She was pinned against the table and heard Luke take two
sharp breaths, then fall silent. Firemen were on the scene
quickly and rescued her other children, but it took some time
and a sledgehammer to free Sandra. The firemen tried without
success to revive Luke. "It was breaking my heart because I
couldn't do anything," she would tell a *Philadelphia Inquirer*
reporter months later. "I couldn't move a muscle. It felt like the
whole house caved in on me, and I could not budge."

Debbie Sherman was pulling into her driveway when she
was hit by the tornado. She grabbed her dog and sped off, trying to outrun the twister. A neighbor said he saw the tornado
suck Debbie's car 200 feet into the air, throw it over a silo, and
slam it into a field, killing her instantly. Sixty-eight-year-old
Stanley Kireta and his wife, Frances, were killed as well. The
local funeral home director told a reporter, "The tornado took
their house, car, and everything, and tossed it over the bank.
We assumed they were in the kitchen and were crushed."

The F4 tornado that blew through Albion completely
wiped out a ten-block section of the town and leveled two
nearby trailer parks, killing a total of nine people.

Just minutes later, about 20 miles away in Pymatuning
State Park, campers looked across the lake and saw a tornado
heading right for them. Some would later say it looked like a
huge white garden hose whipping around in the sky. The
twister slammed into the campground, lifting trailers off the
ground, them slamming them back down. The camp hostess
was killed when a trailer landed right on top of her.

At about the same time, a tornado was spotted a short distance away near Jamestown, headed straight for the town of Atlantic. By the time it reached town, it had grown to an F4. It bent a 300-foot-tall AT&T relay tower and sent it crashing to the ground. Houses, barns, and mobile homes flew through the air. In the cemetery on the outskirts of Atlantic, grave markers were ripped from the ground.

Charles Polley, pastor at the Atlantic Congregational Church, was eating in a restaurant in Meadville when someone came in and said, "A town down the road has just been wiped out by a tornado." Polley rushed toward Atlantic to find only devastation. Houses were reduced to piles of debris, the post office was destroyed, and trees were down everywhere. The only building left standing in Atlantic was Reverend Polley's church. Though there was a gaping hole in the roof and the chalice had been bent at an angle, the large Bible was still sitting on the pulpit, and the church would become a relief center for the entire area for the next several months. Eight people were killed in Atlantic, including a seventy-seven-year-old Amish man who ignored his grandson's pleas to come to the basement, saying the storm would not be that powerful and he wanted to watch it from his front porch.

By this time, the warnings were flying out of every office of the National Weather Service still left with power. The 6 P.M. newscasts were full of news about the tornado touchdowns, but it seemed as though the weather was brightening and the worst might be over. Unfortunately, the largest tornado of the outbreak—an unheard-of F5—was taking aim at the town of Wheatland on the Ohio-Pennsylvania border, having already killed ten people and heavily damaged parts of eastern Ohio.

Helen Duby, the mayor of Wheatland, was sewing in her home at about 7 P.M. while her husband watched the news. He had seen the tornado alerts, but hadn't paid much attention, as the weather outside seemed fine and the storms seemed to be to the north. Duby looked up when she heard the sound of hail hitting the windows, then heard what she thought were planes flying close by. "Those aren't planes, that's a tornado!" her husband yelled, as they both ran for the cellar. When the storm had passed, Mayor Duby looked out down the valley and saw her town in ruins. She headed toward the borough hall, passing destroyed homes, downed power lines and trees, and people wandering around in shock.

What started as a small shower delayed the start of the Little League game in Wheatland, but as the weather grew worse, umpire Dave Kostka, the newlywed, herded the players into the dugouts and told them to get home. Kostka took his niece, Christa, and a friend who needed a ride to his Ford Blazer and took off, trying to beat the weather. They were too late. The first arm of a tornado briefly lifted the Blazer off the ground. Kostka pulled the kids out of the truck, ran to a ditch at the side of the road, and laid on top of them. First the Blazer was sucked into the storm, then Dave Kostka as well. His body was thrown into the wall of a nearby trucking company, and he was killed instantly. The two children with Kostka were only slightly injured, but a six-year-old boy hurrying from the Little League game with his family was also killed.

More than fifty homes in Wheatland were totally destroyed, as were many of the town's businesses. A *Storm Data* publication would later say, "The destruction at Wheatland was so complete that most of the town resembled that of a bombed out battlefield." There were reports of sections of asphalt being peeled off of parking lots. Seven people in Wheatland were killed. As the storm continued east, it passed over the Hermitage Airport, destroying a hangar and several planes. The wing of one plane was later found 10 miles away. After plowing through the small community of Greenfield, the F5 tornado finally died out, after an unbelievable 47-mile-long path of destruction. It had killed a total of eighteen people and injured hundreds more.

Unfortunately, the night wasn't over. One of the strongest tornadoes, another F4, luckily took aim on a largely unpopulated area, hitting the Moshannon and Sproul State Forests of central Pennsylvania in the early evening with winds of up to 250 miles an hour. This storm was not only one of the strongest, it also had the longest track, traveling nearly 70 miles with a damage path that reached 2 miles wide at times. It passed over mountains and crossed the Susquehanna River twice in its ninety-minute run. An estimated 90,000 trees were leveled, at an average rate of 1,000 trees per second, but other than a steel fire tower and one cabin, there was no further damage or loss of life in the parks.

Shortly after 8 P.M., another tornado slammed into the Big Beaver Borough Shopping Plaza just north of Beaver Falls. The roof was ripped off a Jamesway store as customers dove for cover; dozens of pieces of clothing with Jamesway tags still attached would later be found dangling from trees miles away. It took rescue workers several hours to free everyone from the wreckage at the Jamesway. In a state liquor store in the shopping center, a clerk and one customer were crushed to death when all but one of the store's walls collapsed. On the one wall that held, rows and rows of bottles sat untouched on the shelves. This tornado continued on a path paralleling the Pennsylvania Turnpike. Eight women attending a Tupperware party ran for cover in a root cellar. One did not make it; her body would be found in a stream 2 miles away. The twister's final strike was on John's Bar near Evans City, which was crowded on a Friday night. Though the roof was torn off and the front wall collapsed, everyone in the bar survived.

The line of storms weakened as it moved east, but remained strong enough to produce one last tornado, an F1, which touched down at about 9:45 P.M. in the center of the state, causing only minor damage. In all, at least seventeen tornadoes hit that night in Pennsylvania. It would be months before the official tally was determined: In Pennsylvania alone, 65 people were killed and more than 700 injured. In addition, 1,009 homes were destroyed, with damage totaling nearly $400 million. Dead cattle and other animals littered the area's many farms. So many utility lines were down that one phone company worker said, "This will be like rebuilding an entirely new phone system from scratch."

The following morning, the light of day revealed the unbelievable destruction in northwest Pennsylvania. Governor Richard Thornburgh visited the area, saying, "You can't describe devastation like this. You've got to see it. It's unimaginable—houses, buildings. Trailer parks obliterated. They're gone. Try to explain that to someone and they don't believe you." The National Guard patrolled the streets in the hardest-hit towns to prevent looting.

On Sunday, services were held in damaged churches throughout the area, including at Reverend Polley's Congregational Church in Atlantic. In the days that followed, his church would join forces with other congregations to set up a relief center for the surrounding communities. Thousands of members of Amish and Mennonite communities from around the country flocked to the area by bus to help in the rebuilding. One Amish leader explained that his community did not accept federal help because they needed to rebuild quickly. "We all get together . . . everybody brings eats, and we all go to work." In the town of Atlantic alone, an estimated 800 Amish men, women, and children arrived within a week to shovel debris, burn fallen trees, and help rebuild houses and barns. The *Erie Morning News* helped organize a massive food drive and listed offers of housing for people who had lost their homes. The paper was overwhelmed with calls.

The days that followed also produced amazing stories of both damage and survival. A baby ripped from his mother's arms was found in a ditch stripped naked but only slightly injured. A dog that had been tied to a tree disappeared in the twister along with the tree, but was found alive three days later, still tied to a piece of the tree. In Albion, Clark and Janet Snodgrass's refrigerator was sucked out of their house only to be found a quarter of a mile away on the roof of a bank. Some people reported that items from their homes such as pictures, letters, or old checks were found up to 50 miles away.

Many would later question whether communities in the tornadoes' paths had received adequate warning. Though tornado watches had been issued, few were able to hear them. Many homes and communities were without power, and some radio stations were knocked off the air. On a Friday night in early summer, people were busy, driving home from work or settling in for a dinner with their families. Greg Forbes, a meteorologist who analyzed the tornado outbreak for the federal government, would say several months later, "To be truthful, I'm surprised there weren't more fatalities. Houses just aren't built to stand this kind of tornado."

"WE'LL START TO TURN IN"

The Schoolyard Crash That Killed a Senator

1991

John Heinz III was a man on the way up. A hugely popular United States senator from Pennsylvania, he was contemplating a run for the Pennsylvania governorship and, beyond that, some thought perhaps a run for the White House. The sole heir to the H. J. Heinz ketchup and condiment company, he was worth more than $500 million and oversaw the Heinz family's billion-dollar philanthropic foundations. When not at his luxurious Georgetown mansion, he and his elegant, Mozambique-born wife, Teresa, lived in a sprawling farm estate outside of Pittsburgh.

In his years in the U.S. Senate, Heinz, a Republican, became well known for championing the causes of the poor and the elderly. He was remembered by many for standing up on the Senate floor during debate over the Reagan administration's attempts to cut school lunches by, among other things, classifying ketchup as a vegetable and testifying, "Ketchup is a condiment, not a food. And I should know." Having led a seemingly charmed life, many compared Heinz to John F. Kennedy during the Camelot years.

On the morning of April 4, 1991, the 52-year-old Heinz held a news conference in Williamsport, Pennsylvania, then climbed onboard a small rented plane. He was headed to Philadelphia, where he had scheduled the first in a series of hearings called "Bleeding Medicare Dry: The Great Sales Scam," intended to look into the telemarketing trend of targeting medical equipment to Medicare beneficiaries. The Piper Aerostar turboprop carried just Heinz and two pilots on the short hop to the Philadelphia airport.

But just before noon, about 10 miles from the airport, one of the pilots radioed the control tower that he was concerned the landing gear might not be locked in place, since the indicator light in the cockpit was not on. "Right now, we don't have a nose-gear indication," one of the pilots reported. The air controller responded, "Four-five Delta, just let me know if there's anything I can do to help you," then declared an "Alert One," sending word to fire and emergency vehicles that an incoming plane might have to make a belly-landing. A Sun Company helicopter was nearby, flying to company headquarters to take executives to New York City. "Sir, that Aerostar that went past us looks like the gear is down," the pilot told the controller. The Aerostar pilot thanked the crew, but replied that the problem was that they couldn't tell whether the landing gear was locked in place.

The question came from the control tower: "Can you tell me how many souls onboard and your fuel remaining?" The pilot replied there were three onboard—not mentioning that one was a U.S. senator—and that they had plenty of fuel. At 12:03 P.M., the air-traffic controllers suggested that the Piper fly by the control tower for a visual inspection, the standard procedure if there's a possible landing-gear malfunction. The helicopter pilots radioed the tower, offering to fly around the plane to see if the landing gear was down. "Could take a real close look at that if you wanted," the pilot told the control tower.

"Gear looks down. It appears to be normal," was the word from the control tower after the fly-by. The controllers then mentioned that the chopper pilots had offered to take another look. "OK, I would appreciate that," was the response from the pilot. The control tower directed the plane, then flying at about 900 feet, away from the airport. Their path took them over a heavily populated suburban area just outside the Philadelphia city limits. Keeping a close eye on each other, there is no way the pilots could have known they were also flying over an elementary school. "This is seven-eight Sierra. Everything looks good from here," reported the helicopter. "OK, appreciate that," the Piper pilot replied. "We'll start to turn in."

Just beneath them, having finished their lunches, first and second graders from the Merion Elementary School were heading out to the playground to enjoy the sunny, 60-degree day. Postman Dan Matz was making rounds nearby; he remembers looking up and thinking, "That plane is going to hit that helicopter." The two collided at 12:11 P.M.

David Rutenberg had just pushed through the double doors leading to the playground. He told a *Philadelphia Inquirer* reporter years later he remembers hearing a muffled sound, "like a hammer hitting a piece of wood," and then seeing yellow-orange fire and black smoke. He looked up as the twisted helicopter crashed by him, close enough that he could see the two pilots inside.

The debris slammed onto the school grounds—the plane near the drive in front of the stone building, the burning helicopter on the playground out back. All onboard were killed instantly. Rutenberg was set ablaze by burning fuel. He ran back into the building, where he encountered reading teacher Ivy Weeks, who grabbed hold of him and struggled to put out the flames. Custodian John Fowler was talking to the school librarian when he heard the explosion. He ran downstairs "and saw this huge fireball . . . and Ivy with David, trying to extinguish the flames." Fowler ripped off David's burning windbreaker, then wrapped him in his own denim jacket, smothering the flames. Both Weeks and Fowler received minor burns.

The way Rutenberg remembers it, "I think I realized I was on fire, but I don't remember much pain." In fact, he was burned over 68 percent of his body and given just a 30 percent chance of survival. But after numerous surgeries and 170 days in the hospital, Rutenberg returned to Merion Elementary the following September, though he had to wear a bodysuit and a clear face mask.

Two girls on the playground were not that lucky. School psychologist Jill Bressler was driving by the school when the crash occurred. She raced to the playground with debris still falling from the sky toward a girl lying on a burned slope, her clothes in flames. Bressler and another person struggled to put the fire out and resuscitate the girl, but it was too late. Two first graders, Lauren Freundlich and Rachel Blum, died on the playground.

Joe Mandes was overseeing his fifth-grade class. He remembers hearing a sound "like an elephant jumping up and down" and yelling for his students to run from the classroom. Teachers struggled to calm the students, while herding them to safety. Some went into the school auditorium, where the fourth graders had been practicing for their play, *My Country 'Tis of Thee*. Others fled outside to the playing fields, where a firefighter cut a hole in a fence and led the students across the street. School principal Marvin Gold, who called April 4, 1991, the "worst day of my life," lined students up for a headcount and said he felt sick when he determined he was two short. There had been about fifty students outside when the crash occurred, but Gold said that if the accident had occurred just ten minutes later, many more children would have been on the playground.

Almost immediately, panicked parents from the community descended on the scene. Helen Amadio, who had been walking nearby at the time, told reporters, "It was one horrible thing to watch. It exploded like a bomb. Black smoke just poured." David Rutenberg's mother, Rebecca, was having lunch at her kitchen table when her housekeeper called to say she'd heard on the radio about a plane crash at Merion Elementary. "I had a premonition, a bad feeling," Rutenberg recalled. "I just knew something had happened."

Alice Halpern was in her kitchen when she looked out the window and saw a "huge mountain of billowing black smoke and flames" rising from the school grounds. Like many, she had settled in this area specifically because of the school and the close-knit neighborhood. She remembers running from her house and making note of the children who lived in every house she ran by on the way to the school. "We have to find Hannah. We have to find Joanna. We have to find Becca . . ." Both of Halpern's children were unhurt, but she was one of the parents who consoled Rebecca Rutenberg and helped her find her way to the hospital. When she returned home, Halpern found part of the plane's landing gear on her back deck and part of a wing lying in her shrubs. A small black aircraft belt lay on her glass sunroom ceiling.

The school was closed the following day while investigators sifted through the wreckage, and teachers and administrators, still in shock, worked to make the school look like normal for when the children returned. They replaced the carpeting that had burned when David Rutenberg ran back inside; they repainted scorched walls and put in new sod and flowers. Anticipating sending her children back to school the following week, Halpern told a reporter, "Disaster is out there. You have to pray, and you have to hope. You have to be careful, and you have to be lucky."

Many questioned the decision of the pilots to perform a risky maneuver over a populated area, saying the midair check was far more dangerous than a belly landing would have been. A number of aviation experts said the pilots had nothing to gain by checking the landing gear a third time. But all the pilots involved had extensive experience, and government investigators determined that all involved were within acceptable procedures. Nonetheless, nearly two dozen lawsuits were filed against the airplane company and the Sun Company, which owned the helicopter. All were settled out of court.

Flags at the nation's capital flew at half staff in honor of Heinz, whose memorial service was held in Pittsburgh at the Heinz Memorial Chapel. (Teresa Heinz decided not to serve the remainder of her husband's term in the Senate, saying it was more important to be at home with her three sons. She would later remarry another senator—John Kerry of Massachusetts—and become increasingly politically active during Kerry's unsuccessful presidential bid in 2004.)

Just one day after Heinz died, Senator John Tower of Texas was killed in the crash of a commuter plane in Georgia.

The parents of the two girls killed on the playground both established scholarship funds in their daughters' memories. David Rutenberg graduated from the local high school and, ten years later, told a *Philadelphia Inquirer* reporter, "I've never woken up in the middle of the night and gone, 'Oh jeez, why me?' or 'Why did God let this happen?'"

Still a custodian at Merion Elementary ten years after the accident, John Fowler told the same reporter, "Not a day goes by that I don't hear a helicopter and look up and make sure it clears the school. I watch it just to make sure that everything's OK up there. Because you're aware of how quickly an idyllic setting can change."

*The wreckage of USAir Flight 427 litters the ground in Aliquippa, Pennsylvania,
September 9, 1994.* AP/WORLD WIDE PHOTOS/*TRIBUNE REVIEW*/TOD GOMBAR

CHAPTER 19

"THERE WAS NO ONE TO SAVE"

The Crash of USAir Flight 427

1994

The pilots of USAir Flight 427 were in jovial moods as they taxied down the runway of Chicago's O'Hare Airport in the late afternoon of September 8, 1994. It was the last day of their workweek and the atmosphere in the cockpit was good-humored.

But inside the terminal, at least one woman was worried. Carole Griffin Ruzich had driven her husband, Daniel, to the airport for a flight to Pittsburgh. Waiting in the gate, she overheard some passengers as they came off the plane talking about an unusual noise they had heard onboard during their flight from Charlotte, North Carolina. Ruzich was concerned enough that she called US Airway to report what she had heard. When maintenance foreman Gerald Fox answered the phone, he reassured Ruzich that he had two good mechanics on duty who would take care of any problems before the plane took off.

Fox headed outside and climbed the stairs to the plane, known in the company as Ship 513, a seven-year-old Boeing 737 that had logged 23,800 hours in the air. That meant it was a relatively new plane in the US Airway fleet. Fox found Captain Peter Germano and related his conversation with the woman about the strange noise. Germano seemed unconcerned, saying only, "I have a good airplane." He did not mention an incident that had occurred on the leg from Charlotte to Chicago.

On that flight, a first-class passenger named Andrew McKenna had alerted the crew to a strange gurgling sound he had heard above his head. McKenna was a seasoned traveler and explained to a flight attendant that the noise—which he described as sounding like water being forced out of a sink— was different from any he had heard before on his numerous flights. Listening carefully, the flight attendant said she thought the noise was coming from the plane's public address system. She phoned the cockpit, explaining to Germano what the passenger had said. Turning around, the captain noticed that a pilot riding in the cockpit jump seat had his knee pressing on a microphone button. With the move of a knee, the flight continued on to Chicago without any further complaints.

Manning the controls as Flight 427 left O'Hare bound for Pittsburgh were Germano and First Officer Charles Emmett III, who flew the plane out of Jacksonville, Florida, that morning. Both had more than twenty years of flying experience. The flight was packed, mostly with businesspeople, including four employees of U.S. Steel and eight workers for the U.S. Department of Energy returning from a coal conference. Several had been booked on a later flight but changed plans to get home sooner. Janet Stamos, a mother of two and an employee of PNC Bank, in Chicago for computer training, had called her husband in Pittsburgh to say her class ended early and she was rushing to make an earlier flight. Also onboard was an executive from a Chicago radio station, a convicted drug dealer, and the Weavers of Upper St. Clair, Pennsylvania—a family of five returning from the funeral of a nine-year-old cousin. The plane was so full that the family members were scattered in separate seats throughout the coach section.

It was a short hop from Chicago to Pittsburgh—just fifty-five minutes scheduled at 33,000 feet—and the weather was perfect for flying, with sunny skies and temperatures in the seventies. The plane lifted its wheels at O'Hare just after 5 P.M. Chicago time. At the controls, First Officer Emmett relied on the autopilot for most of the flight, and the voice recorder caught the pilots chatting casually with a flight attendant about pretzels and a new drink concoction she had come up with: fruit juice mixed with Diet Sprite. One of the pilots joked that it would taste better with a little dark rum added. As the pilots began their preparations for landing, they were in contact with the control tower in Pittsburgh. Switching on the seat belt sign to prepare for landing, Emmett remembered he hadn't alerted the passengers to prepare for landing.

"Oops, I didn't kiss 'em bye. What was the temperature, 'member?" he asked Germano, then turned on the PA system:

"Folks, from the flight deck, we should be on the ground in 'bout ten more minutes," Emmett said. "Uh, sunny skies, little hazy. Temperatures, temperatures ah, seventy-five degrees. Wind's out of the west around 10 miles per hour. Certainly appreciate you choosing USAir for your travel needs this evening, hope you've enjoyed the flight. Hope you come back and travel with us again. At this time, we'd like to ask our flight attendants, please prepare the cabin for arrival. We'd ask you to check the security of your seat belts. Thank you."

The control tower radioed the pilots about light air traffic in the area—a Delta flight about 4 miles ahead and an Atlantic

Coast Airlines Jetstream commuter plane that had just taken off. "Oh yeah," Emmett responded in a stylized French accent. "I see zuh Jetstream."

Seconds later, the cockpit tapes recorded a "thump," and the plane suddenly rolled to the left. "Whoa," said Germano, as the wings of the 737 leveled off, then rolled to the left again. "Hang on, hang on," Germano repeated four times within four seconds. One of the crew then clicked off the autopilot.

Emmett muttered an expletive that the transcripts recorded as "#," as the pilots struggled to pull up the nose of the plane.

"What the hell is this?" Germano is heard asking.

A computerized collision avoidance system in the cockpit then alerted the pilots to "traffic" twice, likely because the computer spotted the Jetstream commuter plane a few miles away.

"What the . . ." Germano said, as Flight 427 dove toward the ground at 240 miles an hour.

"Oh God! Oh God!" Germano cried, then shouted to controllers: "427 emergency!" Emmett is heard cursing repeatedly as the plane fell, while Germano calls "Pull!" several times.

At the airport, controller Richard Fuga heard the shouts of the pilots as he watched the plane's altitude reading on his radar screen turn to "XXX," indicating the plane was falling at such a high speed that his computer could not register it.

The last words on the tape are Emmett's—"God! . . . No!"

Flight 427 plowed into a hillside just twenty-eight seconds after the first "thump" of trouble in the cockpit. All 132 people onboard were killed instantly.

It was 7:03 P.M. Eastern Time, and soccer games were well underway on the fields in Hopewell Township, about 6 miles west of the Pittsburgh airport. "Look at that airplane!" someone on one of the fields shouted, as the 737 plummeted. In a nearby shopping center, Amy Giza had just climbed into her car when her six-year-old son said, "Mommy, that airplane just fell out of the sky."

George David was cutting flowers in his yard when he heard the roar of airplane engines, then a loud explosion. Though trees blocked his view, David clearly saw a huge fireball rising from the gravel road that led to his neighbor's house. Within minutes, at least seventy-five people had called 911; the first was entered in the log as "Hysterical Caller." At fire stations throughout the area, the call came in—"Zulu at Pittsburgh International Airport," meaning a disaster with at least twenty fatalities. More than forty fire trucks, police cars, and ambulances descended on the scene. Captain James Rock was one of the first. As he neared the wreckage, he saw luggage, twisted metal, and mangled airplane seats. He saw parts of human bodies. The field was also littered with thousands and thousands of copies of *BusinessWeek* magazine that had been on the plane headed to subscribers in the Carolinas. But the force of the impact had shattered the plane into so many small pieces that a police officer at the site wondered, "Where's the plane?"

Retired Beaver County Emergency Management Director Russ Chiodo said later, "We tried to save somebody, but there was no saving anyone. There was no one to save."

Once the fire was out, the gruesome task of recovering victims for identification began. A temporary morgue was set up in a giant hangar at the Pittsburgh airport's Air Force Reserve Station. Over the next days, some 2,000 workers combed over the crash site; many would later be treated for post-traumatic stress disorder. Led by forensic pathologist Dr. Karl E. Williams, a team of coroners worked to identify the victims. Long before DNA identification was possible, they relied on dental records or fingerprints for some, a piece of jewelry and a hip replacement joint for others. In the end, Williams and his team were proud to have identified 125 of those onboard Flight 427.

It was clear from the beginning that this was going to be a difficult crash investigation. Tom Haueter, the lead investigator, said, "Flight 427, at that time, was the most fragmented aircraft I had ever seen. There was nothing there." Two months after the crash, investigators from the National Transportation Safety Board (NTSB) first heard the cockpit tape recordings. "This crew had no idea what happened," one said. "They never realized what was going on."

It would take five years—the longest investigation in NTSB history—to determine what caused USAir 427 to fall from the sky. In 1999, investigators announced that a faulty rudder design in the 737 was to blame; when hot fluid passed through a cold rudder control system, the rudder went in exactly the opposite direction from what the pilot was commanding. The Federal Aviation Administration ordered Boeing to redesign the rudder system, which it did at a cost of $1 billion. "There's more than a million people who ride in 737s daily," said Captain John Cox, a US Airway pilot who chairs a safety group of the Air Line Pilots Association. "All of those people are in a safer aircraft."

The crash of Flight 427 also changed the way airlines communicate with the families of victims of airline accidents. Many relatives complained that as they rushed to the Pittsburgh airport, they were simply herded into a lounge and told only that there had been an accident with fatalities. They were then left alone. All through the night, no one provided the families with information about victims or how many had died. Other panicked relatives calling the airline were told by US Airway agents that they couldn't release any details yet, but would call back when they could. US Airway initially told Tammy Bober that her brother was on Flight 427, then called back to say that he was not. But the family suspected the worst. "It took seven hours. It was 2:30 A.M. before we had actual confirmation," Bober said. "We knew he was on the plane. He was supposed to be home and he wasn't."

In the morning, some distraught family members were allowed to drive home alone from the airport. As a result of the airline's handling of the families after the crash, Congress later passed the Disaster Family Assistance Act. "I can't think of one accident that had more impact on the NTSB, on the aviation industry, and more importantly, on how families of all disasters are treated worldwide than the Pittsburgh accident," said Jim Hall, chairman of the NTSB at the time.

Most of the victim's families settled lawsuits against US Airway for between $2 million to $4 million. One of the largest, $7.2 million, went to relatives of the Weaver family— the mother, father, and three children who were killed.

The families oversaw the construction of a granite memorial at the crash site, which reads, "This site is dedicated in fond and loving memory to the 132 passengers and crew of USAir Flight 427 which crashed here at 7:03 P.M. on September 8, 1994." Every once in a while, someone in the area will unearth small pieces of metal or twisted wires and lay them on top of the memorial.

"A TICKING TIME BOMB"

First the Snow, Then the Floods
1996

Pennsylvania thought it had survived the "storm of the century." When the March blizzard blew through in 1993, dumping several feet of snow over much of the eastern United States, everyone said it was a once-in-a-century event. That storm produced the widest swath of snow on record, shutting down every major airport on the East Coast, killing more than 200 people, and leaving millions without power. Twenty-five inches of snow fell in Pittsburgh, where temperatures hovered in the single digits for several days. Several weeks later, when spring arrived, many people breathed a sigh of relief that they wouldn't see a storm like that again in their lifetimes.

That's why just three years later, weather forecasters were rubbing their eyes in disbelief as they studied the computer printouts in early January. Another nor'easter packing heavy snowfall was headed toward Pennsylvania. As it turned out, record snows were just the beginning of a one-two punch that would devastate much of the state.

At first the weather models looked like Pennsylvania might be spared. But by Friday, January 5, the storm appeared to be taking dead-aim on the Philadelphia area. One television station called its weatherman vacationing in Cancun, Mexico, and told him to catch the next flight out. By the time the first flakes fell on Sunday, the state thought it was pretty well prepared. No one had any idea how bad it would get. The snow started falling early Sunday morning and by the time it finally came to a halt the next day, the city of Philadelphia lay buried under a record 30.7 inches of snow. Some parts of the state in the higher elevations were hit with more than 3 feet. At times, the blinding snow fell at a rate of several inches an hour.

Much of the state was paralyzed, with the worst reserved for the eastern half, typical of a nor'easter. In and around Philadelphia, the snow was falling too hard and fast to clear the streets. In some communities, the snowplows gave up altogether. Train lines and airports shut down; even the U.S. Postal Service had to admit that 2.5 feet of snow *could* keep carriers from the swift completion of their appointed rounds . . . at least for a day. Virtually all businesses shut down; in one twenty-four-hour convenience store, workers unable to leave the store resorted to eating food from the shelves.

Safety became an obvious, immediate concern. Though fire officials urged people to dig out the hydrants near their homes, several fatal fires were reported during the storm and in the days immediately following. The fire trucks simply couldn't get to some streets, and even when they could, they couldn't find the hydrants. There were other storm-related fatalities in Philadelphia as well. Sixty-four-year-old Elizabeth Dalessandro was found frozen Sunday evening just outside her home in the height of the storm. She had gone out to buy groceries for herself and her husband, who was homebound with Parkinson's disease.

Several additional deaths would be blamed on the storm in the several days that followed. At least three people suffered fatal heart attacks while shoveling snow, and one man died of carbon monoxide poisoning. Joseph Dilulio was found by neighbors in his car, which was running in his driveway encased in snow. In another instance, four-year-old Rickiya Daniels was also overcome by carbon monoxide fumes when she was strapped in a car seat with the car engine running for warmth while her grandmother shoveled snow off the car. After four fruitless calls to 911, the grandmother ran to a nearby fire station, and paramedics were able to revive the girl. An elderly homeless man froze to the death on a sidewalk; thousands of other homeless crowded into the city's shelters.

The process of plowing streets was nearly impossible. Plows would clear one block and dump the mounds of snow only to find that they had blocked an intersection. In Philadelphia, twenty-ton city trucks were called into action to carry loads of snow to the Market Street Bridge and unceremoniously dump their contents into the Schuylkill River. That worked for a while, until the Coast Guard ordered the city to stop the dumping out of concern the snow might dam the river altogether.

Many streets were clogged with cars that had become stuck or broken down. In one case, a city bus full of passengers was stuck for seventeen hours after a car in front of the bus broke down. Someone on the bus told a reporter the car's driver had shrugged and said, "I only paid $500 for it," before walking off. Though several riders trudged off on their own, others gave up when they sank waist-deep in snow on the sidewalk. Six passengers and two drivers were marooned on the bus overnight, helped considerably by Jack Kinslow, a nearby resident who brought blankets to the passengers. His wife cooked up some pasta, brewed a pot of coffee, and took her best china onto the bus to serve dinner to those who were stranded. "It turned into a neighborhood effort, with people taking care of them," she said.

There were many other reports of neighbors helping neighbors, and citizens going the extra mile to help out. Some doctors used their skis to get to work to relieve exhausted colleagues, while the National Guard and police were called upon to deliver blood to area hospitals. Several hospitals reported that people with four-wheel-drive vehicles just arrived at their doors, volunteering to help bring patients in. At one hospital, a pregnant woman with labor pains was brought in by firefighters onboard a full-scale ladder truck. In Lancaster County, a pregnant woman was pulled on a sled by a snowmobile to the hospital, arriving just in time to give birth. In Philadelphia, a paramedic on the way to help a woman in labor had to push stranded motorists out of the way, then walk several blocks on foot. He assisted Candice Wiggins in a breech birth in her living room, talked through by an obstetrician on a portable phone.

The entire region was brought to a standstill; some schools and businesses remained closed for a week. Pennsylvania Governor Tom Ridge appealed to Washington for federal help, saying the snowstorm was "as much of a tragedy and disaster for us as a hurricane or earthquake in other parts of this country." The city of Philadelphia was left with a $23 million cleanup bill, and statewide, the government estimated that the storm resulted in $750 million in costs and lost sales, particularly in the thirty-two hours after the blizzard when state roads remained closed.

Still, by the following week, the state had struggled back to life. The roads were cleared, stores and businesses reopened, and things returned to normal—or what passed for normal when there was 2 feet of snow on the ground. . . . Until January 18, just ten days after the blizzard, when the temperatures started to climb.

On January 18 and 19, thermometers read above sixty degrees, and all that snow began to melt quickly, compounded by heavy rains that arrived along with the warm front. What started as a blizzard was about to become a disastrous flood.

While many Pennsylvanians were delighted with the mid-January warm weather after such a cold, snowy month, the National Weather Service saw reason for concern. By Tuesday, January 16, with rain in the forecast and temperatures on the rise, the service was issuing advisories about possible flooding. In the early morning hours of Friday, the 19th, the rains began, dumping up to 5 inches in some parts of the state in just a matter of hours.

In Tionesta in northwestern Pennsylvania, Mark Cook's telephone rang at 5 A.M. Workers next to his motel and campground had smelled propane. It was too dark for Cook to see anything outside, but what he heard worried him. The nearby Allegheny River was running through his campground. Shortly after 6 A.M., Tom Cunningham, the mayor of the small town of Hyndman, in Bedford County, got into his car and eased his way into hubcap-deep water. Next thing he knew, Cunningham said, a wave rolled down the street and swept over the hood of his Plymouth Neon.

Throughout much of the state, people reported waking up Friday morning and not believing their eyes when they looked outside—all of the snow was gone. In State College, workers at the National Weather Service office estimated that nearly 2 feet of snow had melted in less than twelve hours.

Throughout the northern part of the state, the heavy, warm rains were melting mounds of snow and breaking up ice jams in rivers and streams. The snowpack "got so soppy that when the rain hit, it was like hitting a saturated sponge," said John McSparren, the chief engineer at the Susquehanna River Basin Commission in Harrisburg. "Everything ran off. It was incredible how it all came at once."

Early Friday morning, Betsy Rupp was driving across a small bridge in Bedford County, when the water engulfed her Chevy Malibu, sweeping it off the road and into a tree. When Rupp tried to open the door, it wouldn't budge. Panicked, she unbuckled her nineteen-month-old daughter from her car seat, rolled down her window and put her daughter on the car's roof, and screamed for help. Nearby, a man heard her screams and slogged through chest-high water to carry the girl to safety. He then returned for Rupp, and by the time they had reached dry ground, Rupp's car was completely under water. Another man in Bedford County was rescued by a helicopter from a tree he had climbed after his pickup truck was flooded.

As the rains continued, jams in rivers began to break up, with huge chunks of ice breaking off and heading downstream, taking with them a growing amount of debris. An employee at an Army Corps of Engineers lock in Armstrong County called the National Weather Service to report the Allegheny River had already risen 9 feet. By early afternoon, it was clear the city of Pittsburgh was in trouble. The head of the city's Emergency Operations Center decided it was time to open the "War Room," a high-tech command center for city disasters that wasn't even finished yet.

Things were getting worse further to the west as well. Along the Juniata River near Altoona, seventeen-year-old Walter McChessney was caught in a flood, clinging to a fence. A rescuer on a jet ski tried to rescue him but flipped over just as McChessney was carried downstream. He grabbed onto a tree and a National Guard helicopter was called, but just as the chopper lowered a rescue harness, the boy slipped under the water. His body was found sixteen hours later.

In Lycoming County near Williamsport, residents reported that a 4-foot wall of water roared down the Lycoming Creek after an ice jam broke loose upstream. The water flipped cars and smashed into businesses, destroying more than 130 automobiles at one car dealership. Seventy-seven-year-old Frank Kangenski and his wife were trying to outrace the rising water when their car stalled out in a cornfield. Both were killed. Thirty-eight-year-old Mary Ann Blair drowned after she was swept off the roof of her mobile home along the creek. Sixty-eight-year-old John Keck was killed when his car was swept off a bridge along Route 14. In all, six of the nineteen deaths attributed to the floods in the state occurred in Lycoming County. A local police chief reported to state authorities that evening, "There is devastation all over. . . . We have approximately three-and-a-half miles of creek where all the homes are destroyed."

By early evening, flood warnings were going out to businesses in Pittsburgh, where the Allegheny, Monongahela, and Ohio Rivers converge at what is known in the city as the Point. Water was already pouring into the basement of the Fulton Building downtown, and several streets had been closed. Late that evening, security guards at the Andy Warhol Museum called the city emergency center to report water was filling the basement. A fire chief dispatched to the scene reported the water was rising so quickly he couldn't get to the building. A National Weather Service forecaster upped the flood estimates for Pittsburgh, saying "The Monongahela River came up like the infamous bat out of hell."

Shortly after midnight, as many as twenty barges broke loose upstream near Oakmont and plowed down the Allegheny, slamming into bridges along the way. In the darkness, inspectors had no way to know whether the bridges were damaged and were forced to close them all until daybreak. As the barges continued downstream, they were joined by pleasure boats, some still attached to docks that had broken loose. Referring to the huge ice floe, a security official said, "Whatever it hits on the way down is officially closed." There was nothing the Coast Guard could do but watch. Chief Mike Vesco told a Pittsburgh reporter, "The water's so high that tow boats can't get under the bridges and the ice is so thick that most boats can't get through it."

As the floods worsened in the overnight hours, communities stepped up evacuations. In McKeesport, the boiler room flooded at a housing project, forcing a middle-of-the-night evacuation of 450 residents. Several municipal water plants had to stop pumping because their plants were under water. The Allegheny County Sanitary Authority had to shut down its huge sewage treatment plant, which resulted in raw sewage being dumped directly into the rivers.

During the overnight hours in the northeastern town of Wilkes-Barre, city officials were keeping a close eye on the city's dikes as the levels of the Susquehanna River began to rise quickly. Memories of the widespread flooding that followed Hurricane Agnes in 1972 were still fresh in the minds of many, and people were understandably nervous. "Back in '72 I found a coffin in my backyard," one resident told a Philadelphia reporter. "This time the river looked just as bad. It was swirling." The National Guard was called in to shore up the dikes, and police went door to door telling people in low-lying areas to evacuate their homes. By midmorning, the call had come to evacuate a total of 100,000 people. (The dikes held, and the river crested at 5:30 P.M., 1 foot short of topping over. Though many homes suffered damage, city officials credited the improved dike system with preventing disastrous flooding.)

To the southwest, the same Susquehanna waters sent nearly 8,000 Harrisburg residents to higher ground. Among them were Pennsylvania Governor Tom Ridge and his family, who were told to look for other sleeping quarters that night when waters began to pour into the basement of the Governor's Mansion. Governor Ridge's wife, Michele, helped staff members carry antiques and furniture to safety on the mansion's second floor, then the family evacuated to the State Police Academy in Hershey. Nearby, officials tried to figure out what to do about a 124-car freight train that had become frozen on tracks along the Susquehanna. All train service between Harrisburg and Philadelphia was halted.

The Pittsburgh rivers finally crested at about 10 A.M. Saturday at an official reading of 34.61 feet. Standing on the banks of a river in Pittsburgh, one person watching the ice chunks float by said, "Look at how fast that ice is moving. The river looks like a field of speeding, white rocks." A resident of McKees Rocks near Pittsburgh watched as the remains of a marina dock floated by, including an ice machine, gas pump, and a picnic table with its umbrella still poking up. One local official summed up the flooding by saying, "We had three rivers that went nuts at the same time."

At Three Rivers Stadium in Pittsburgh, the home of the Super Bowl–bound Steelers, water had risen up to the entrance gates. The team was forced to flee its home stadium and prepare for its big game a week away on higher ground. (The Steelers lost to Dallas the following Sunday.) Point State Park, with its famous Fort Pitt battlement outlines, lay beneath a field of water, ice, and debris.

The PECO energy company was forced to declare an "unusual event" at the Peach Bottom Nuclear Power Plant Saturday at 5:10 P.M., when water rose to 111 feet in its adjacent cooling pond. Crews at PECO's Conowingo Dam rushed to open what floodgates they could. A company spokesperson said that at its peak, the Susquehanna was flowing through the floodgates at about six million gallons per second, twelve times higher than is usual for January. Had the water risen just 1 foot more, PECO would have had to shut down the reactors.

Many local communities declared states of emergency during the floods, but it was not necessary for Pennsylvania Governor Ridge to take the same action—the state was still under an official emergency declaration from the snowstorm ten days earlier. President Clinton declared residents of all sixty-seven counties in the state eligible for emergency relief funds. It was the first time in history that the entire state had been hit with a weather disaster. "There has never been an occasion of such widespread flooding," said John Comey of the Pennsylvania Emergency Management Agency. "In a normal disaster, conditions are very concentrated."

Statewide, the government estimated there were $1 billion in damages and costs caused by the blizzard and the flooding. More than 11,000 homes were destroyed or suffered major damage, and more than 1,500 bridges and roads needed major repair. Ninety-nine deaths in the state were blamed on the combined storm, eighty from the blizzard and nineteen in the floods. The day after the floods, Governor Ridge described the snowstorms of early January as "the ticking time bomb, and it went off with these incredible thaws."

"IN THE COCKPIT! IF WE DON'T, WE'LL DIE"

The Crash of United Flight 93

(2001)

On the morning of September 11, 2001, with the horrified eyes of the world watching the unfolding nightmare at the World Trade Center and the Pentagon, an unknown life-and-death drama was taking place in the skies above western Pennsylvania. Three planes, hijacked by terrorists, had already wrought their destruction in New York and in Virginia, just outside of Washington, D.C. A fourth hijacked plane reversed course over Pennsylvania and was believed to be headed for the White House or the U.S. Capitol in Washington. Onboard United Flight 93 were thirty-seven passengers, two pilots, and five flight attendants who made the heroic decision to fight back against the four terrorists who had commandeered their plane.

When Flight 93 lifted off from the Newark airport at 8:42 A.M. on the morning of September 11, several people onboard were concluding their first-ever visits to New York. They surely were enjoying one last look at the city's striking skyline, dominated by the twin towers of the World Trade Center, clearly visible to the right on this clear day as the plane left the runway. One passenger, Christine Snyder, had made an excursion to lower Manhattan the day before just to have a drink with a friend at the Windows on the World restaurant at the top of the Trade Center.

With only 37 passengers onboard a plane with a capacity of 182, the crew was anticipating a relaxed flight to San Francisco. "I've got an easy day," flight attendant CeeCee Lyles told her husband by phone shortly before takeoff. Captain Jason Dahl had traded a trip later in the month to pilot Flight 93 so he could take his wife on a weekend trip to London to celebrate their fifth wedding anniversary.

Dahl had piloted the Boeing 757 nearly up to its cruising altitude of 35,000 feet when an alert appeared from dispatchers on the ground: "Beware cockpit intrusion. Confirm operations are normal." United operators on the ground were sending that message to every flight in the air, a reaction to the hijackings that were unfolding in New York and Washington. A member of the cockpit crew typed back, "Confirmed." Controllers in the air control tower in Cleveland had fielded questions from several other pilots about the vague reports of trouble in New York, but no such inquiry came from the crew of Flight 93, which announced its arrival in Cleveland air space with a pleasant "good morning."

It was a routine handoff, with the Cleveland controllers alerting Dahl to another plane 12 miles away. But it soon became clear there was trouble in the cockpit on Flight 93. Muffled sounds of a struggle and someone screaming "Hey!" filled the Cleveland control room. Confused, a controller radioed, "Did somebody call Cleveland?" After a half minute of silence, the sounds of chaos from the cockpit could once again be heard over the air traffic control frequency, one of the pilots apparently having thought to push the button on the audio panel. There was yelling, someone screaming repeatedly "Get out of here!" But the pilots were not responding to repeated calls from the air controllers. Just after 9:30 A.M., the controllers' worst fears were confirmed when they heard voices in Arabic from inside the cockpit, then a transmission intended for the passengers of Flight 93: "Ladies and gentlemen, here is the captain, please sit down. Keep remaining sitting. We have a bomb onboard. So sit."

By this time, those in the cabin were well aware of the turmoil onboard. Several minutes earlier, four men had stood up, wrapped red bandanas around their heads and pulled knives. One said he had a bomb strapped to his body. The hijackers quickly herded most of the passengers toward the rear of the plane, where word of the situation began to spread quickly, as passengers pulled out their cell phones or used the Airfones onboard.

Deena Burnett was making breakfast for her children in San Ramon, California, when her phone rang. "I'm on United Flight 93 from Newark to San Francisco," whispered her husband, Tom. "The plane has been hijacked. We are in the air. They've already knifed a guy. There is a bomb onboard. Call the authorities." Deena immediately called 911, and was patched through to the FBI. The agent misunderstood her, asking if her husband's flight was one of the planes that had hit the World Trade Center. "No, this is another flight," she replied.

During this time, a female voice on the cockpit recorder, presumably that of a flight attendant, was heard pleading, "Don't, don't. Please, I don't want to die." Investigators later determined that flight attendant Debbie Welsh and both pilots were likely stabbed or had their throats slashed early in the takeover. The female voice pleaded "I don't want to die" one last time on the tape before there were sounds of female cries, followed by a hijacker saying in Arabic, "Everything is fine. I finished." Even though most of the passengers were in the rear of the plane, some said they could see bodies lying just outside the cockpit. One of the flight attendants in the back of the cabin managed to get through to the United Maintenance Center in San Francisco to inform the airline about the hijacking. She told them one hijacker had a bomb strapped on his body and another was holding a knife to members of the flight crew.

At about 9:35, the plane changed direction, making a 180-degree turn. That put Flight 93 directly on a course for Washington, D.C. Air traffic controllers also noticed that the plane's altitude was rising and falling erratically. At one point, the plane climbed to 41,000 feet, 6,000 feet above its assigned altitude.

At 9:40, a message from the hijackers, believed to be pilot Ziad Samir Jarrah, was once again picked up over the radio: "Here's the captain. I would like to tell you all to remain seated. We have a bomb onboard, and we are going back to the airport. And we have our demands. So please remain quiet." The controllers immediately radioed back: "United 93, understand you have a bomb onboard. Go ahead," but there was no response. Shortly thereafter, the transponder signal from Flight 93 was turned off. "This green knob?" asked one of the hijackers on the tape. "Yes that's the one," came the response in Arabic.

Without the transponder, air traffic controllers could no longer receive data directly from the plane. Instead, they had to rely on radar and visual sightings from other planes. Although they could no longer determine the plane's altitude, the controllers could tell that the aircraft's speed was fluctuating wildly, from between 400 to 600 miles per hour. Experts now say this was an indication that the hijackers were struggling to control the 757, none of them having had experience flying commercial planes.

As more passengers made contact with loved ones, there was a growing sense of urgency as those on the plane learned about the attacks in New York and Washington. Tom Burnett placed another call to his wife, Deena, who remembers telling him, "They're taking airplanes and hitting landmarks all up and down the East Coast." Burnett responded: "Oh my God, it's a suicide mission." Shortly after 9:40, passenger Mark Bingham called his mother. "I want to let you know that I love you," he said. "I'm on a flight from Newark to San Francisco and there are three guys who have taken over the plane and they say they have a bomb." (Bingham had been the last person to board the flight. He had overslept that morning and had been rushed to the airport by a friend. The flight attendants had to reopen the locked doors to let him on just before Flight 93 pushed back from the gate. As the plane taxied, he had called his friend and said, "Thanks for driving so crazy to get me here. I'm in first class, drinking a glass of orange juice.")

Along with updates of what was happening in New York and Washington, the telephone conversations with those onboard Flight 93 consisted of messages of love and excruciating good-byes. In a call to upstate New York, thirty-one-year-old sales manager Jeremy Glick told his wife, Lyz, "I need you to be happy, and I will respect any decisions that you make." Twenty-seven-year-old Honor Elizabeth Wainio reached her stepmother, Esther Heymann, in Baltimore, saying she had called to say good-bye. "We don't know how this is going to turn out," Heymann said, trying to reassure her stepdaughter. "I've got my arms around you." The two spoke for eleven minutes, with Heymann telling Wainio to breathe deeply and concentrate on the clear blue sky outside. Near the end of the call, Wainio told her stepmother, "It makes me so sad that it's going to be so much harder for you all than it is for me."

Lauren Grandcolas was unable to reach her husband, Jack, in San Rafael, California. She left a message on his answering machine: "Sweetie, I love you. There's a little problem with the plane. I'm totally fine. I love you more than anything, just know that. I'm comfortable and I'm okay for now."

Todd Beamer, a thirty-two-year-old account manager for the Oracle Corporation from Cranbury, New Jersey, was having difficulty using the plane's Airfone, so he was routed through to a Verizon customer service center. As soon he told the operator he was on a flight that had been hijacked, he was patched through to Lisa Jefferson, a Verizon supervisor, who stayed on the phone with Beamer for the duration of the flight. He told Jefferson he was sitting next to a flight attendant and could see three hijackers, all armed with knives. One hijacker guarding the passengers in the rear of the plane insisted he had a bomb. At one point, Beamer shouted into the phone, "Oh, we're going down!" Then after a pause, "No, we're OK. I think we're turning around. I really don't know where we are going. Oh, Jesus, please help us." Beamer gave Jefferson his home phone number and made her promise that she would call his wife and their two sons and tell them he loved them.

At about the same time, Tom Burnett made a third call to his wife. "We're going to do something. I'll call you back." The passengers were starting to plan. As it became clear that the hijackers intended to crash the plane into a building, those onboard felt they had no choice but to act. Jeremy Glick told his wife the passengers had taken a vote to see if they should try to take over the plane, with all of the men voting to attack the hijackers. Despite the terror surrounding him, Glick also managed to make a joke to his wife. When she asked what they could use to fight back, he responded, "We just had breakfast and we have our butter knives."

As it turned out, although there were only thirty-seven passengers on Flight 93, several of them were well suited to the challenge that lay before them. Mark Bingham was a rugby player; Tom Burnett had been a quarterback in college; Jeremy Glick was a judo champion; forty-two-year-old Louis Nacke was a weightlifter; and sixty-year-old William Cashman was a former paratrooper; he was also an ironworker who had helped install iron support structures during the construction of the World Trade Center. Even one of the flight attendants, thirty-three-year-old mother of two CeeCee Lyles, had spent six years as a police officer in Florida. Also among the passengers were Don Greene, a professional pilot, and Andrew Garcia, a former flight controller.

The frantic calls from Flight 93 began to spell out a plan. Flight attendant Sandy Bradshaw told her husband she and several passengers were in the rear galley filling pitchers with boiling water to throw on the hijackers. In his final call to his wife at 9:55 A.M., Tom Burnett said, "There's three of us who are going to do something about it." When his wife objected and urged him to just sit down and be quiet, Burnett responded, "If they're going to crash this plane into the ground, we're going to have to do something. It's up to us. I think we can do it." On the phone at 9:58 A.M., Sandy Bradshaw told her husband, "Everyone's running to first class. I've got to go."

At about this time, Todd Beamer ended his long conversation with Lisa Jefferson. During the thirteen minutes they were
on the line together, Beamer had provided specific information
about what was happening on the plane to Jefferson, who was
also in contact with the FBI. The two had also taken time to say
the Lord's Prayer and recite together the words of the Twenty-
third Psalm. Jefferson said she could hear others around
Beamer also repeating the comforting words of the Psalm.
Beamer told her at the end that he was going to have to "go out
on faith" because the plan was for passengers to "jump" the
hijacker in the back of the plane. Jefferson said she could
already hear sounds of an "awful commotion" in the background with shouting and someone screaming, "Oh my God
. . . God help us." Beamer left the phone line connected, allowing Jefferson to hear his last words to nearby passengers: "Are
you ready guys? Let's roll."

Investigators now believe that a group of passengers ran
down the aisle toward the cockpit, using a food cart to ram the
cockpit door. Sounds on the voice recorder at 9:57 appeared to be
breaking glass. "Is there something? A fight?" a hijacker asked
in Arabic. Someone shouted, "In the cockpit! In the cockpit!" In
Arabic, the hijackers told each other to hold the door. "They want
to get in here. Hold from the inside," one said, while outside
someone shouted, "Let's get them." The hijackers were also
heard on the recording praying "Allah o akbar"—God is great.

A hijacker could also be heard on the recording suggesting
shutting off the oxygen flow to the cabin, while another asked,
"Should we finish?" Another answered, "Not yet." One
hijacker proposed using the plane's fire axe to scare the passengers. As the sound of the passengers became clearer on the
recording, someone could be heard in English saying, "Give it

to me!" Another voice cried, "I'm injured." Then a voice could be heard saying, "Roll it up, lift it up."

Just before 10 A.M., CeeCee Lyles was still on the phone with her husband. "It feels like the plane's going down," she said. "I think they're going to do it. They're forcing their way into the cockpit." A few minutes later, she screamed, "They're doing it! They're doing it! They're doing it!" Her husband later said that after that, he heard more screams in the background, then a "whooshing sound, a sound like wind," then more screaming, before the call was disconnected.

Investigators believe that at this point, the hijackers were rolling the plane sharply back and forth, trying to throw off the passenger revolt. The pilot of a small plane in the area was alerted by a flight controller to look for a plane nearby. He reported seeing Flight 93 about 3 miles away, rocking back and forth three or four times. Witnesses on the ground also said they saw a passenger plane flying at about 2,000 feet, dipping its wings sharply to the right and then the left. Rodney Peterson, an auto mechanic in Boswell, saw the plane that day. He later said, "If they were fighting with the hijackers, I guarantee it happened right here. It dipped left and dipped right. No plane that big flies like that."

Just after 10 A.M., someone in the cockpit asked, "Is that it? Shall we finish it off?" Another voice answered, "No. Not yet. When they all come, we finish it off." The pilot then began to pitch the nose of the plane up and down. The tapes record a passenger's voice saying, "In the cockpit! If we don't, we'll die," followed by the sounds of more crashing metal and glass. Another voice says, "Roll it!"

By 10:01, the rocking of the plane had stopped. Voices in the cockpit repeated "Allah o akbar! Allah o akbar!" Someone

Firefighters and emergency personnel investigate the scene of the crash of a United Airlines Boeing 757 about 80 miles southeast of Pittsburgh. AP/WIDE WORLD PHOTOS/*TRIBUNE-REVIEW*, TOD GOMBAR

asked, "Is that it? I mean, shall we put it down?" to which another hijacker responded, "Yes, put it in it, and pull it down."

Although there were no phone calls from Flight 93 after 10 A.M., some phones were left on and recorded sounds in the background—screams, followed by silence, followed by a mechanical noise, more screams, then more silence. Loud wind sounds can be heard at the end of the cockpit voice recording. Some family members who heard the tape concluded that the passengers had indeed wrested the controls away from the hijackers. The official conclusion was that there was no way to know for sure.

Flight 93 was going 580 miles an hour when it plowed into an empty field near Shanksville, Pennsylvania, in Somerset

County, at 10:03 A.M. Somerset County resident Lee Purbaugh
said he was 300 yards from the plane when it crashed. "There
was an incredibly loud rumbling sound and there it was, right
there, right above my head—maybe 50 feet up," he told
reporters at the scene. "I saw it rock from side to side then, suddenly, it dipped and dived, nose first, with a huge explosion, into
the ground. I knew immediately that no one could possibly have
survived." At a United systems operations center near Chicago,
the radar track of Flight 93 disappeared. A director called an airport manager in nearby Johnstown, asking if he could see anything. The manager reported back that he saw a plume of dark
smoke about 30 miles away. Terry Shaffer, the Shanksville fire

*Each of these patriotic angels bears the name of a person whose life
was lost on Flight 93.* LIBRARY OF CONGRESS, PRINTS & PHOTOGRAPHS DIVISION, PHOTOGRAPH BY
CAROL M. HIGHSMITH, LC-DIG-PPMSCA-02123

chief, was one of the first on the scene. "You wanted to do something," he said, "but there was nothing to be done."

The plane crashed just short of the town of Shanksville and a school filled with nearly 500 students. It was only 124 miles—about twenty minutes of flying time—from Washington, D.C.

At a memorial service near the crash site several days later, Pennsylvania Governor Tom Ridge, who would later become the country's first Director of Homeland Security, said that by fighting back, those onboard the plane had saved hundreds, if not thousands, of lives. "They sacrificed themselves for others—the ultimate sacrifice," Ridge declared. "What appears to be a charred smoldering hole in the ground is truly and really a monument to heroism." A national memorial for the passengers and crew is planned for the serene Pennsylvania field where Flight 93 went down.

"WE'RE ALL NINE HERE"

Quecreek Mine Rescue

2002

Just ten months later and 10 miles away from the site of the 9/11 crash of United Flight 93, the eyes of the nation were once again focused on a drama playing out in Somerset County, Pennsylvania. A series of underground mine tunnels runs from the reclaimed strip mine where Flight 93 crashed that horrible day to what was known as the Quecreek Mine, a two-year-old project run by the Black Wolf Coal Company. Stretching beneath the farms of Lincoln Township were deep veins of rich bituminous coal. The process of getting that valuable coal out of the ground had changed tremendously since the early days of coal mining that had fueled Pennsylvania's industrial growth in the nineteenth and early twentieth centuries. The work was now highly mechanized and much safer than in the days when mining disasters could claim hundreds of lives. But in the Pennsylvania counties where generations of families had worked the mines, everyone was still painfully aware that mining was a treacherous way to make a living.

At Quecreek, three shifts worked around the clock more than 200 feet underground, coaxing the coal out of the earth. On Wednesday, July 24, 2002, the two 9-man crews of the late shift had been at work since 3 P.M. in different sections of the mine. One was charged with working on a coal seam about 1.5 miles into the mine, 245 feet underground; the nine men in that crew had close to 200 years of combined experience working underground.

Just before 9 P.M., with two hours left in his shift, forty-one-year-old Mark "Moe" Popernack was at the controls of what was called a continuous miner, a sixty-ton machine with one hundred "teeth" that grind the coal out of the veins and shoot it onto a waiting shuttle. Popernack chipped away at a wall of coal he believed to be hundreds of feet thick. That's what his map told him. But in fact, the wall was narrow—leading to the remains of an abandoned mine that in the fifty years since it was closed had slowly filled with water. Once the powerful machine drilled through the wall, it unleashed a torrent of more than 70 million gallons of water into the Quecreek mine. Popernack jumped away from the machine into a crosscut as the water almost instantly covered it with orangish, murky water.

"Everybody out! We hit an old section! There's a lot of water!" screamed Thomas Foy, a fifty-two-year-old miner who worked on the crew with his son-in-law.

Separated from his coworkers by a growing river of water, Popernack hollered to forty-nine-year-old Dennis Hall, who was behind him operating an electric-powered shuttle car that hauled away the coal. Known as "Harpo," Hall had been a miner for thirty years and knew well the dangers of the job. He had been trapped for an hour in a cave-in early in his career and had once had his jaw broken by a drill that broke loose. "Harpo! Get the hell out! Get out now!" Popernack hollered. Hall sped off, but made it only 200 feet before the water knocked out his shuttle's power.

In the deafening roar of the water in the first seconds, it was difficult for the miners to hear the shouts of warning. But the gushing water was warning enough, and the men began a desperate fight to escape. Randy Fogle, the forty-four-year-old crew foreman, had the presence of mind to yell at Hall to use a nearby phone to warn the second crew working in another part of the mine. The son and grandson of miners, Fogle was a lifelong miner who also had training as an emergency medical technician. Hall quickly picked up the phone, reaching at first someone on the surface, then finally a member of the second crew working several thousand feet away. "We got major water coming in . . . Get the f— out now!" he cried.

Once that crew was able to make its way to safety, slogging through tunnels quickly filling with water, it was no time before word spread about the disaster unfolding underground, and emergency crews rushed to the scene.

In the mine, the eight miners were separated from Popernack by a river of water. They found each other by looking for their head lamps, but there was no way they could reach Popernack. "We both knowed there was no chance that I could get him with me," Fogle recalled. "I locked eyes with him. He shook his head. 'Go without me,' he was saying."

The eight miners fell back on their safety training. Hurrying as best they could through the cramped tunnels, which were filling with dirty water, they gathered at a tunnel where a conveyor belt moved the coal out of the mine. With water rising around them, they had to hold onto the coal conveyor for support. Stooped in passageways just 4.5 feet high, they struggled to make progress in the rising water, which quickly rose to their necks. Soon they had no choice but to climb on the conveyor itself and crawl. The two youngest miners, thirty-one-year-old Blaine Mayhugh, Tom Foy's son-in-law, and thirty-six-year-old John Phillippi were in the lead, and had made it about 2,000 feet down the conveyor when their helmet lamps shone on the danger ahead. Just 100 feet ahead, the water was so high it was lapping at the roof. They yelled to the others to turn back. "We're in trouble," Foy said to his son-in-law. "I know," Mayhugh replied. "I'm too young to die. I'm not afraid to but I got two little kids. This ain't the way for us to go."

Above ground, rescue efforts were kicking into high gear. Dave Rebuck, the owner of the Black Wolf Coal Company, had rushed to the mine and alerted state and federal officials about the breach. Joe Sbaffoni, Pennsylvania's deep-mining expert, quickly met with other experts, poring over maps before hurrying to Quecreek, where rescue equipment was starting to arrive. The police were alerted just before 10 P.M., and they began notifying the families of the miners about what had happened. There was little to tell the panicked family members that gathered at the Sipesville firehouse. No one knew whether the miners had been able to find a safe place to hide from the rushing waters in the mine. The first step for rescuers was to find out where the men would have retreated. Common sense told them the miners would work their way to high ground to keep their heads above water. Then they used global positioning satellites to determine where the best place was to drill in an air pipe. They settled on Bill Arnold's dairy farm.

It was an arduous effort underground for the miners to find that high ground. After having to turn around from the conveyor belt, they veered into several cross shafts where the water was just too high to proceed. Fighting through the torrents, the miners now had to walk forward while craning their necks back to keep their mouths above water. Finally, they made their way to an area tall enough that they didn't have to struggle to keep their heads above water. There, Fogle used his mason's hammer, hoping to break through a cement block wall into another passageway. When he grew too exhausted, the other miners took turns swinging the hammer, but the water was rising, and having made no progress, the men moved on. They slowly worked their way back toward where they had been working when the breach occurred, which was high and still above water.

All this time, Moe Popernack had been stranded alone. He had begun to think he would die in the mine when he saw a light across the still-raging river of water. It was the helmet lamp of his crewmate John Phillippi, who had set out to search for him. They yelled back and forth about how to rescue Popernack. It was Fogle who came up with the idea of using a small highlift called a scooper. He maneuvered the scooper as far into the water as he could, then yelled to Popernack to jump into the bucket, carefully easing his crewmate back to safety. The nine miners were together again; Robert Pugh remembers thinking "We're all going to drown together or we're all going to get out of this mess somehow." And shortly after that, they heard the sound of drilling from above.

As a first line of offense, the emergency crews above knew they had to get fresh air to the miners. While some worked to locate a drill capable of digging a hole big enough to raise the men through, others began drilling a hole down to the area they had determined was the high ground. At about 5 A.M. Thursday, a drill broke through from above, followed by a pipe that brought a welcome blast of warm, fresh air. And just in time. The miners had been working hard to build walls with cement blocks that could serve as dikes and hold the water back. But it was hard work in low-oxygen air, and it was taking its toll. Several of the men had started vomiting, and some were too exhausted to continue working.

The fresh air from above brought renewed hope—the res-cuers had figured out where they were. Crews pumped in 190-degree compressed air, hoping to offset the effects of being trapped in what was estimated to be 55-degree water. But they also knew that as well as pumping air in, they had to find a way to pump water out if the miners were going to survive. Middle-of-the-night calls went out to anyone with a pump and a drill that could reach 300 feet underground. Somerset County emergency dispatcher Jeremy Coughenour remembered that his old Sunday school teacher ran a drilling business. A call to her home brought Judy Bird, her husband, and three daugh-ters to the mine, where they got to work right away.

With the air pipe in place, the miners realized they might have a way to communicate with workers aboveground. They started tapping hard on the pipe—nine bangs, hoping to signal that there were nine men alive. When the tapping was picked up above, hopes soared for those on the rescue crew. Although unsure about the meaning of the nine taps, rescuers at least knew someone had survived, giving a renewed urgency to their efforts. And time was of the essence, as monitors in the mine showed the area where the miners had sought refuge would be underwater in about an hour. A mine ventilation expert at the site came up with the suggestion to create an air pocket in the mine by sealing the hole around the air pipe and pumping in compressed air at such high pressure that it actually prevented the water from rising. It was an idea that had never been used in the United States, but it worked to a point, slowing the water's progress. That bought some time for bringing in ten additional drills to allow for water pumps. Five big pumps were on their way from Bridgeport, Connecticut.

There was still the question of how to bring the miners up, assuming they survived. One of the drill companies at the site proposed using what it called a "super drill," which utilized a 1,500-pound bit—the only machine powerful enough to create a chute wide enough to bring the miners to safety. The problem was the super drill was in Clarksburg, West Virginia, hours away.

By noon Thursday, the miners had completed work on four cinder block walls, but their hopes were dashed again as water overtook them while they were working on a fifth. "The water's just pouring in," John Unger remembered. "And Randy was trying to throw block up. It was hopeless." They had no choice but to move again—further away from the airshaft—to the highest ground possible. There the only thing they could do was wait. Randy Fogle didn't pull any punches; he told them that by his estimates, they had just about one hour before the water reached them. When that happened, they would all be dead.

The news brought a solemn realism to the group. Some said silent prayers, others cried. Blaine Mayhugh took a piece of cardboard off the ground and wrote a note to his wife and kids. He put it in a white plastic bucket, and offered his pen to the others. "My note was short," said Moe Popernack. "I made it short because I wanted everybody to have time to write their note and the water was coming really fast." After each one had written their notes, they snapped on the bucket's airtight lid, sealed it with electrical tape, and tied it to a machine so it wouldn't float away. Some of the miners used a cable to tie their belts together, thinking that way it would be easier for their bodies to be found. In this somber mood, there was still room for dark humor. When one miner asked, "How are we going to die?" Unger responded, "I could hit you on the head with a rock or else you could just drown." The chuckle couldn't hide the truth, though. "You're looking at everybody and you think, 'Well, we're all going to die together,'" Unger said. "'This is it. This is the bottom line.'"

The miners said they lost track of time, unsure whether it was day or night. They mostly sat in silence; some prayed. About an hour passed, but still the water had not reached the miners. Fogle had made several trips down to check on the water level when he came back and said "I think the water stopped rising." They put a stick in the water to keep track of the level, and before long, it was clear the water was dropping—though very slowly. Once again, a jolt of hope spread among the miners. They resumed pounding on the roof. They turned off their helmet lamps so they wouldn't drain the batteries, switching one on only every ten minutes to make sure the water level hadn't risen. That left them in total darkness, and the most pressing concern became the cold. They were soaking wet, and the temperature in the mine was in the fifties. They tried sitting back-to-back or laying close to each other under a tarp. "When somebody would start shivering, teeth chattering, we'd get that guy in the middle and we'd all sit around him," forty-nine-year-old Ron Hileman said. But not much helped. Except for Fogle's news that the water still seemed to be creeping down slightly.

As Thursday evening fell, spirits were high among the rescuers. The pumps were working, and the super drill had arrived at the scene, rushed up from Virginia with a police escort. By 7:30 P.M., the drill was at work, and the process of digging a 29-inch wide, 240-foot tunnel to the miners began. It had been hours since rescuers had heard any tapping from the mine, but they did not give up hope. Until about 2 A.M. Friday, when the drill bit broke. It had chewed its way 105 feet into the ground, almost halfway to the miners, but was going nowhere until the bit could be replaced. Retrieving the broken bit out of the ground was a problem in and of itself. When Governor Mark Schweiker announced the setback on a morning news program Friday, it was a low point for anxious family members who had been camped out at the fire hall. Schweiker went from the interview to meet with the families, where he assured them the workers were doing everything humanly possible to get the rescue back on track.

Rescuers turned to Frank Stockdale, plant manager of Star Iron Works in Big Run, Jefferson County, to construct a tool capable of fishing out the broken drill bit. In just three hours, Stockdale managed to fashion a "fishing hook" that was airlifted to the site by a National Guard helicopter. The hook pulled the 1,500-pound bit out of the tunnel at about 4 P.M. Friday. After a fourteen-hour shutdown, the rescuers resumed their work.

In the cold and dark below, the miners waited. Some tried to sleep; others discussed what they would do if they ever got out. They found Dennis Hall's lunch pail in the water near them, and shared a corned beef sandwich and a Pepsi. They had also found twelve gallons of distilled water normally used for machine batteries. Robert Pugh shared his tin of Timberwolf snuff. When the sound of the drilling above stopped, Hall remembers thinking, "Dear God, they gave up on us," but others speculated about a broken bit and tried to keep up their spirits.

With the super drill working again, rescuers knew there were other concerns. The drill had to slow its pace during the final 50 feet to protect the air pocket they had created. If they went too quickly, they worried that all of the air would rush out, potentially allowing water to flood the space. They also worried about what a sudden drop in pressure would do to the miners, who were at risk of "the bends," the same condition that can affect scuba divers. A doctor arranged for ten portable hyperbaric chambers to be delivered to the site so the miners could be immediately treated for decompression illness. Others worked to devise an airlock for the top of the escape tunnel, fashioning a 40-foot-long tube to prevent the pressurized air from leaking out once the escape capsule could be lowered to the miners.

Finally, at 10:15 P.M. Saturday, the rescue drill broke through into the roof of the mine. The drill operator pumped his fist in the air in victory; there was euphoria at the rescue site and at the firehouse when the news reached the anxious and exhausted families. Ironically, the miners didn't know about the breakthrough right away. They had been making sporadic trips down to the air pipe to pound on the pipe and check on the water. Before long, Ron Hileman and Tom Foy returned from such a trip shouting, "We found the hole! Everyone get down there!"

The miners immediately started banging on the pipe and yelling through the tunnel. A man named Rob Zaremski, whose company had invented a small two-way communication probe, had been called to the site. Zaremski snaked the CON-SPACE Rescue Probe through the air pipe, equipped with a child's glow stick so the miners could see it in the dark. All the drills and pumps were shut off, so for the first time in days, there was silence at the rescue site. As the probe descended, he called out: "Stay where you are. Can you hear me?" Eventually, unmistakably, he heard the response he had been waiting for: "We can hear you."

"Are you the trapped miners?"

"Yes, we are."

"Are you OK? How many are you?"

"We're all nine here."

While getting the rescue capsule ready to go, workers peppered the miners with questions. A doctor took medical histories of each of the men. Hall learned that the other crew in the mines on Wednesday had made it out safely, thanks to his call. And rescuers were getting good news about conditions in the mine. The air pressure had dropped, so the air lock would not be needed.

Finally, the 8.5-foot capsule was lowered into the tunnel, with lantern lights leading the way. It carried supplies the miners had requested: flashlights, cap lamps, some candy bars, blankets, raincoats, drinking water, and snuff and chewing tobacco.

Everyone agreed Randy Fogle should be the first one up. He had a heart condition and had been suffering from chest pains. Fogle emerged from the tunnel at 12:50 A.M. Sunday, covered with coal dust, to the sounds of cheering. After that, the miners were told to come up in order from the heaviest to lightest, so they could help each other get into the capsule.

One by one, they were pulled to safety. Danny Sacco, head of one of the medical teams, stood at the top of the tunnel and greeted each by saying, "welcome home." Robert Pugh came out of the capsule dizzy from having consumed too much snuff and candy. He said all the lights and cheering "gave me

Despite freezing temperatures, hunger, and fatigue, all nine miners were lifted up to safety in this 8.5-foot capsule.

PENNSYLVANIA DEPARTMENT OF ENVIRONMENTAL PROTECTION

a feeling like the Steelers won the Super Bowl." Moe Poper-nack—the last man out—was pulled out at 2:45 A.M. Around the country and the world, people woke up Sunday morning to learn that the miners had been rescued.

Though all were taken to hospitals where they were finally reunited with their families, only three were admitted for treatment. Doctors could tell the miners were doing okay when they started asking for chewing tobacco and beer. While the hospital relented on the tobacco, the beer had to wait.

The nine became instant celebrities. The following week they received a visit from President George W. Bush. There were parades, private jets to NASCAR races, television appearances, and magazine spreads. Each received $150,000 from the Walt Disney Company for a television movie about the rescue. Together, they published a book about their experience. Only one—Randy Fogle—has returned to mining. "I had to go back. I have to support a family, and I had to do it for the industry to show people mining is safe." While some of the others indicated they were willing to go back down into the mines, they said they promised their families on the day they were rescued that their mining days were over.

None of the miners have told anyone what they wrote in their farewell notes to their families, and they never plan to. Instead, they said they planned to take the bucket back down into the mine and entomb it in the walls of coal.

Bibliography

The Yellow Fever Epidemic

"Destroying Angel: Benjamin Rush, Yellow Fever and the Birth of Modern Medicine." Online book by Bob Arnebeck. www.geocities.com/bobarnebeck/fever1793.html.

Eyewitness to History Web site. "Yellow Fever Attacks Philadelphia, 1793," www.eyewitnesstohistory.com (2005).

Lewallan, James Bradford. "Dr. Benjamin Rush: Progressive Patriot in the War Against the Yellow Fever Epidemic of the 1790s." www.samford.edu/schools/ artsci/scs/lewallan.htm. 2001.

Powell, J. H. *Bring Out Your Dead: The Great Plague of Yellow Fever in Philadelphia in 1793.* Philadelphia, Pa: University of Pennsylvania Press, 1949.

The Great Pittsburgh Fire

"Hell with the Lid Off: 150 Years Ago, A Third of Pittsburgh Went Up in Flames." *Pittsburgh Post–Gazette*, April 9, 1995.

The Mystery. "Pittsburg in Ruins!!" April 16, 1845. Carnegie Library of Pittsburgh: www.clpgh.org/exhibit/neighborhoods/downtown/down_n10a.html.

Pittsburgh City Paper: www.pittsburghcitypaper.ws/prev/archives/newsarch/ask/ask01/ya72501.html.

The Camp Hill and Shohola Collisions

Camp Hill

Adams, Charles J., III, and Seibold, David J. *Great Train Wrecks of Eastern Pennsylvania.* Reading, Pa.: Exeter House Books. 1992.

"The Great Train Wreck of 1856." www.reference.com/browse/
    wiki/Fort_Washington,_Pennsylvania.
New York Daily Times. "Appalling Calamity." July 18, 1856.
———. "The Disaster on the North Pennsylvania Railroad." July 19,
    1856.

Shohola

"Brass Buttons and Leather Boots." Sullivan County Civil War Cen-
    tennial Commission. New York Historical Society. 1963.
"The Great Shohola Train Wreck." www.catskillarchive.com/
    rrextra/eriepage.html.
"The Great Shohola Train Wreck." www.shohola.com/trainwreck/.
New York Tribune. "A Fearful Railroad Collision." July 19, 1864.
"Shohola Train Wreck: Civil War Disaster" Elmira Prison Camp
    Online Library. www.angelfire.com/ny5/elmiraprison/
    boydarticle.html.

The Johnstown Flood

Johnstown Area Heritage Association. www.jaha.org/Flood
    Museum/history.html.
"Johnstown Flood." www.pahighways.com/features/johnstown
    flood.html.
McCullough, David G. *The Johnstown Flood.* New York: Simon &
    Schuster, 1968.
McGough, Dr. Michael R. *The 1889 Flood in Johnstown, Pennsylvania.*
    Gettysburg, Pa.: Thomas Publications, 2002.
Philadelphia Inquirer. "Worse and Worse: the Latest from Johns-
    town Swells the List." June 3, 1889.

Coal Mine Calamities

Harwick

"And Then a Hero Comes Along." www.sitnews.us/BobCiminel/ 101804_focb.html.

Carnegie Hero Fund Commission. www.carnegiehero.org.

New York Times. "Explosion Death List 174." January 28, 1904.

———. "Miners Entombed." January 26, 1904.

Darr

"Darr Mine Disaster." http://patheoldminer.rootsweb.com/ darr2.html.

New York Times. "Federal Experts Direct Rescuers." December 22, 1907.

The Washington Penna Reporter. "Only Six Bodies are Recovered at Darr." December 20, 1907. www.usmra.com/saxsewell/darr.htm.

Marianna

New York Times. "125 Are Killed in Model Mine." November 29, 1908.

———. "Take 52 Bodies from Model Mine." November 30, 1908.

Washington Observer archives: www.usmra.com/saxsewell/ marianna.htm.

Harrisburg Rail Yard Explosion

Adams, Charles J., III, and Seibold, David J. *Great Train Wrecks of Eastern Pennsylvania.* Reading, Pa.: Exeter House Books. 1992.

Harrisburg Patriot-News. "Stories Multiply for Disasters." March 7, 2004.

New York Times. "Thrilling Incidents in Night of Terror." May 12, 1905.

Pennsylvania Railroad Technical & Historical Society:
      www.prrths.com/Hagley/PRR1905%20Mar%2005.pdf.
Philadelphia Inquirer. "Twenty Known Dead, Probably 140 Hurt in
      Wreck and Explosion Which Tore and Cremated Express." May
      12, 1905.
————. "Survivors Relate Awful Experience." May 12, 1905.

The Boyertown Opera House Fire

"100 Dead in Theatre Fire." *New York Times,* January 14, 1908.
"Opera House Fire was Berks' Greatest Tragedy." *Reading Eagle* and
      Reading Times, September 24, 2001.
Schneider, Mary Jane. *A Town in Tragedy: The Boyertown Opera
      House Fire.* Volume II. Boyertown, Pa.: MJS Publications. 1992.
————. *Midwinter Mourning: the Boyertown Opera House Fire.*
      Volume 1. Boyertown, Pa.: MJS Publications. 1991.
"Survivors Awful Fight For Life." *Philadelphia Inquirer,* January 15,
      1908.

Eddystone and Oakdale Explosions

Eddystone

"Eddystone Explosion." Ridley Township History. www.ridley
      townshiphistory.com/eddystone_history.htm.
New York Times. "See Plot in Powder Blow-Up." April 11, 1917.
Philadelphia Inquirer. "119 Killed, 150 Injured, Majority Women, By
      Explosion Laid to Plotters in Plant of Eddystone Ammunition
      Corporation." April 11, 1917.
————. "Hero In Rescue Work Is Injured by Shell." April 11, 1917.
Warfel, Louis J. *My Book of Old Chester.* www.oldchesterpa.com/
      history_warfel.htm

Oakdale

Historical Society of Carnegie, Pa. www.rootsweb.com/~pahsc.

New York Times. "Known Dead by TNT Explosion Now 56." May 20, 1918.

———. "200 Die as TNT Plant is Wiped Out by Explosion." May 19, 1918.

Philadelphia Inquirer. "200 Dead, 300 Hurt in Munitions Explosion." May 19, 1918.

The Chester Bridge Collapse

"Chester, Pa: Tragedies; Third Street Bridge Collapse" www.old chesterpa.com/tragedies_third_st_bridge_collapse.htm.

New York Times. "Faulty Plate Cause of Chester Disaster." September 12, 1921.

———. "34 Persons Drown as Crowded Bridge Falls Into River." September 11, 1921.

Philadelphia Inquirer. "At Least 25 Persons Drown at Chester When Bridge Collapses Under Big Crowd." September 11, 1921.

The Crash of the Congressional Limited

Adams, Charles J., III, and Seibold, David J. *Great Train Wrecks of Eastern Pennsylvania.* Reading, Pa.: Exeter House Books. 1992.

New York Times. "Survivors Tell Scenes of Horror." September 7, 1943.

———. "Survivors of Wreck Tell How Servicemen Helped." September 7, 1943.

Philadelphia Inquirer. "Girl with Legs Trapped Refuses to Give Up." September 7, 1943.

———. "75 Killed, 120 Injured in Wreck of Congressional Limited Here." September 7, 1943.

———. "Train Wreck Victims Confused and Helpless." September
     7, 1943.
"The Wreck of the Congressional Limited." www.amusement
     parknostalgia.com/congress.html.

The Donora Smog Crisis

Davis, Devra. *When Smoke Ran Like Water: Tales of Environmental
     Deception and the Battle Against Pollution.* New York, NY: Basic
     Books. 2002.
New York Times. "1948 Donora Smog Killed 20; London Toll was
     4,000 in '52." November 26, 1966.
Philadelphia Inquirer. "Smog Dissolves After Death Toll Hits 20 in
     Donora." November 4, 1948.
———. "20 Died. The Government Took Heed. In 1948, a Killer
     Fog Spurred Air Cleanup." October 28, 1998. www.dep.state
     .pa.us/dep/Rachel_Carson/dead20.htm.
Pittsburgh Post-Gazette. "Cleaner Air is Legacy Left by Donora's
     Killer 1948 Smog." October 29, 1998. www.dep.state.pa.us/
     dep/Rachel_Carson/clean_air_legacy.htm.
Pittsburgh Tribune-Review. "Donora's Killer Smog Noted at 50." Octo-
     ber 25, 1998. www.dep.state.pa.us/dep/Rachel_Carson/
     killer_smog.htm.

The Wreck of the Phillies Special

Adams, Charles J., III, and Seibold, David J. *Great Train Wrecks of
     Eastern Pennsylvania.* Reading, Pa: Exeter House Books. 1992.
New York Times. "Rail Crash Toll is Revised to 19." July 30, 1962.
Philadelphia Inquirer. "1,000 Rush to Scene After Tragedy Strikes."
     July 29, 1962.
———. "23 Killed in PRR 'Phillies Special.'" July 29, 1962.

"Steelton, Pa. Accident Report." Keystone Crossings: http://kc.pennsyrr.com/passops/steeltonwreck.html.

Underground Centralia Fires

"Centralia's Mine Fire History." www.offroaders.com/album/ centralia/the-story.htm.
"Fire in the Hole." *Smithsonian Magazine,* May 2005. www.smithsonianmagazine.com/issues/2005/may/firehole .php?page=1.
"The Great Centralia Coal Fire." *Harper's Magazine,* February 2004.
Jacobs, Renée. *Slow Burn.* Philadelphia: University of Pennsylvania Press. 1986.
Philadelphia Inquirer. "As Centralia's Fires Smolder, Residents Hang On." March 18, 2001.
———. "Why Residents Remain in the Firetrap of Centralia." April 19, 1983.

Hurricane Agnes

"Agnes Caused Major Floods in 1972." www.usatoday.com/weather/ whagnes.htm.
"Hurricane Agnes Hits the Eastern Seaboard." www.trivia-library .com/a/hurricane-agnes-hits-the-eastern-seaboard.htm.
Nese, John, and Schwartz, Glenn. *The Philadelphia Area Weather Book.* Philadelphia: Temple University Press. 2002.
Philadelphia Inquirer. "Shapps Share Misery; Mansion Under Water." June 24, 1972.
———. "State Staggers Under New Storm." June 24, 1972.
"Storms of the Century." www.weather.com/newscenter/special reports/sotc/storm10/agnes/page1.html.

Legionnaire's Disease Outbreak

"Memories of a Deadly Gathering." www.q-net.net.au/~legion/
Legionnaires_Disease_Worlds_First_Outbreak.htm.
New York Times. "Legionnaire's Disease: 5 Years Later the Mystery Is
All But Gone." January 19, 1982.
Philadelphia Inquirer. "After a Quarter Century, Outbreak Still Holds
Mystery." June 13, 2002.
————. "Hotel, Another Victim of Legion Disease, Sells Belong-
ings." July 13, 1978.
Pittsburgh Tribune-Review. "Medical Mystery: Survivors Struggle
With Memories." July 21, 1996.

Three Mile Island

"Fact Sheet on the Accident at Three Mile Island." www.nrc.gov.
"Inside TMI: Minute by Minute." www.kd4dcy.net/tmi.
"Meltdown at Three Mile Island."www.pbs.org/wgbh/amex/three/
filmmore/index.html.
Philadelphia Inquirer. "Unsure, Afraid, Residents Flee Unseen
Threat." March 31, 1979.
USA Today. "Three Mile Island Twenty Years Later." March 28,
1999.
Walker, J. Samuel. *Three Mile Island: A Nuclear Crisis in Historical
Perspective.* Berkeley: University of California Press. 2004.

Tornado Outbreak

"May 31, 1985, Tornado Outbreak." www.pahighways.com/features/
may31tornadoes.html.
"Memorable Tornado Outbreak of May 31, 1985." www.angelfire
.com/pa/pawx/053185.html.

New York Times. "Death and Debris Shatter a Quiet Evening." June
  1, 1985.
Philadelphia Inquirer. "And I Just Sat There Stunned." June 1, 1985.
———. "Tornadoes Rip Northwest Pa." June 1, 1985.
———. "The Victims Came From All Walks of Life." June 3, 1985.

The Schoolyard Crash That Killed a Senator

"The Death of Senator John Heinz." www.newsmakingnews.com/
  vm,deadly,1991,10,15,04,pt2.htm.
Philadelphia Inquirer. "Counting Blessing Amid Pain the Day after
  the Tragedy." April 7, 1991.
———. "A Decade of Healing." April 1, 2001
———. "L. Merion Crash Tape Released." April 24, 2001
———. "A Sunny Spring Thursday Explodes in a Ball of Fire," April
  5, 1991

The Crash of USAir Flight 427

Adair, Bill. *The Mystery of Flight 427: Inside a Crash Investigation.*
  Washington, D.C.: Smithsonian Institution Press. 2002.
New York Times. "For Many on Jet, Day Began with Routine Business and Ended with Terror." September 10, 1994.
———. "USAir Transcript Shows Plunge Was a Complete Sur-
  prise." January 24, 1995.
Pittsburgh Tribune-Review. "Remembering Flight 427." September 5,
  2004.
"28 Seconds: The Mystery of US/Air Flight 427." www.sptimes
  .com/28-seconds/zulu1.html.

First the Snow, Then the Floods

Nese, John, and Schwartz, Glenn. *The Philadelphia Area Weather Book*. Philadelphia: Temple University Press. 2002.

Philadelphia Inquirer archives from January 1996, including:

———. "Flood Unrivaled in Breadth." January 28, 1996.

———. "Mother Nature Couldn't Stop Babies." January 9, 1996.

———. "Region Emerging from Blizzard." January 10, 1996.

Pittsburgh Post-Gazette. "Meltdown: The Diary of a Flood." January 22, 1996.

The Crash of United Flight 93

"Complete 911 Timeline, United Airlines Flight 93." www.cooperative research.org/timeline.jsp?timeline=complete_911_timeline&day _of_9/11=ua93.

Longman, Jere. *Among the Heroes: United Flight 93 and the Passengers and Crew Who Fought Back*. New York: Harper Collins. 2002.

"On tape, passengers heard trying to retake cockpit." www.cnn .com/2006/LAW/04/12/moussaoui.trial/index.html.

Pittsburgh Post-Gazette. "Flight 93: Forty lives, one destiny." October 28, 2001.

Quecreek Mine Rescue

Our Story: 77 Hours that Tested Our Friendship and Our Faith. By the Quecreek Miners (as told to Jeff Goodell). New York: Hyperion. 2002.

Philadelphia Inquirer. "Two Years After Mine Rescue, Impact Sstill Felt." July 25, 2004.

Pittsburgh Post-Gazette. "'All Nine Alive!' The Story of the Quecreek Mine Rescue." August 4, 2002.

"Quecreek Mine Accident." www.pahighways.com/features/quecreek.html.

About the Author

Freelance writer and editor Karen Ivory began her career as a broadcast journalist, writing and producing for ABC and CBS television affiliates in St. Louis, New York, and Philadelphia. She is the author of *Philadelphia Off the Beaten Path,* and co-author of *Eight Great American Rail Journeys: A Travel Guide.* In addition, she has worked on *Globe Trekker's World: A Month-by-Month Guide to What's on in the World . . . and When; Main Streets & Back Roads of New England;* and *National Geographic* guides to *America's Public Gardens, America's Great Houses,* and *Best Birdwatching Sites.* She lives in Philadelphia with her husband and two daughters.

THE INSIDER'S SOURCE